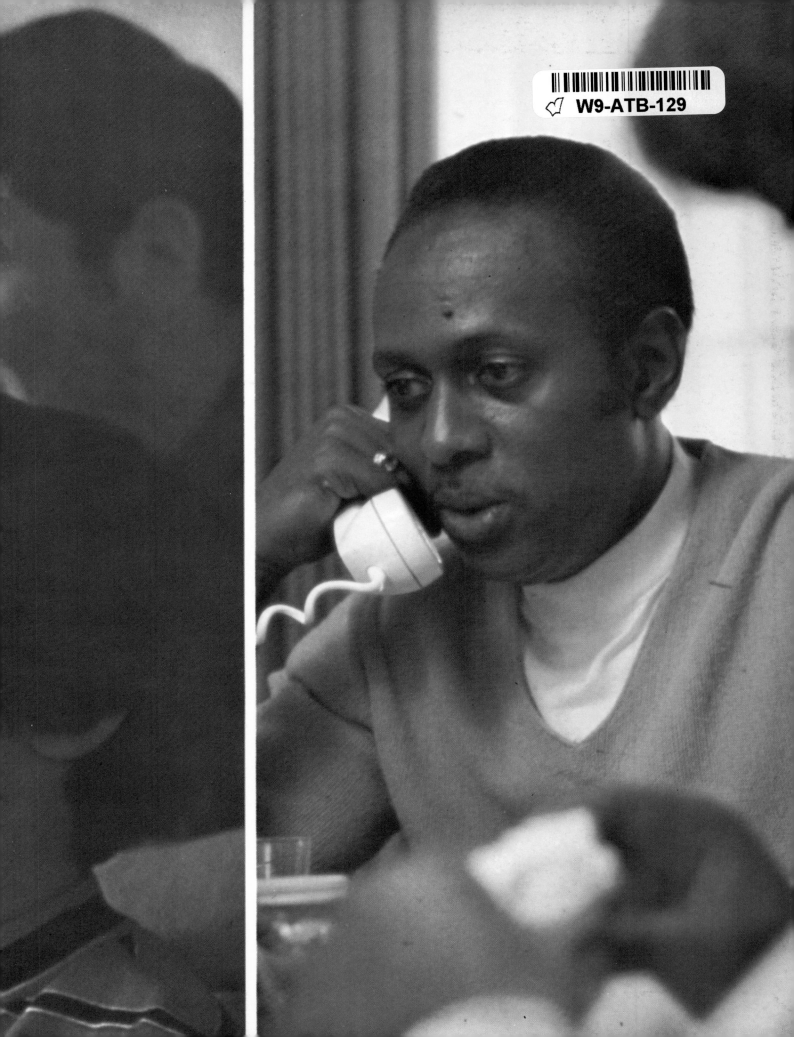

There is a season for everything, a time for every occupation under heaven:

A time for giving birth,

a time for dying;

a time for planting,

a time for uprooting what has been planted.

A time for killing,

a time for healing;

a time for knocking down,

a time for building.

A time for tears,

a time for laughter;

a time for mourning,

a time for dancing.

A time for throwing stones away,

a time for gathering them up;

a time for embracing,

a time to refrain from embracing.

A time for searching,

a time for losing;

a time for keeping,

a time for throwing away.

A time for tearing,

a time for sewing;

a time for keeping silent,

a time for speaking.

A time for loving,

a time for hating;

a time for war,

a time for peace.   Ecclesiastes 3, 1-8

Published by Pastoral Educational Services/NCRD
National Catholic Reading Distributors
400 Sette Drive, Paramus, New Jersey 07652

Executive Director: Rev. Thomas E. Comber, C.S.P.
Coordinating Director of Pastoral Educational Services:
Joseph W. Nash
Director of Distribution Services: Mr. Stanley Truskowski

Division of Paulist Press
Publisher: Rev. John Carr

Editorial Director: Joseph W. Nash
Design: Ron Cutro Associates
Photographic Consultant: Ed Lettau

NIHIL OBSTAT:
Rev. Msgr. George Shea
Censor Librorum

IMPRIMATUR:
✠ Thomas A. Boland, S.T.D.
Archbishop of Newark, N. J.

July 21, 1969

Library of Congress
Catalog Card Number: 75-96134

Printed and bound in the
United States of America

BELIEF IN HUMAN LIFE

REV. ANTHONY T. PADOVANO

Section		Chapter		Page
1	**HUMAN LIFE**	1	THERE IS A TIME FOR GIVING BIRTH	6
		2	THERE IS A TIME FOR KEEPING	12
		3	THERE IS A TIME FOR SPEAKING	18
2	**HUMAN LOVE**	4	THERE IS A TIME FOR LOVING	28
		5	THERE IS A TIME FOR LAUGHTER	38
		6	THERE IS A TIME FOR TEARS	48
		7	THERE IS A TIME FOR BUILDING	54
		8	THERE IS A TIME FOR KEEPING SILENT	60
3	**HUMAN DEATH**	9	THERE IS A TIME FOR THROWING STONES AWAY	66
		10	THERE IS A TIME FOR HEALING	70
		11	THERE IS A TIME FOR WAR	78
		12	THERE IS A TIME FOR PEACE	81
APPENDIX			COMPLETE TEXT OF PASTORAL LETTER: Human Life in Our Day	83

Introductory Note

It is no small thing to believe.

Because many of us learned something about faith when we were children, there is a tendency to equate faith with that which is simple, relatively easy, fundamentally effortless. There is, of course, a sense in which this is true. Faith is closely allied with and always inseparable from life. And life, we know, can be simple, relatively easy, fundamentally effortless. One, all of a sudden, finds himself alive and continues to live unless something drastic is done to interrupt a seemingly inevitable process. In saying this much of life, however, we have omitted further aspects of the drama and mystery of living.

Life includes moments when there is no simple way, when the burden of living becomes so heavy that we feel we can no longer continue, when the sheer effort of performing even elementary tasks to preserve life seems more than we can manage. On one day, life is a beautiful, tender, perfect experience. We appreciate everything and everyone, forgiving our enemies and congratulating our friends. On such a day, it is difficult to know why we ever thought life was difficult. On another day, however, nothing is right and no one can help. We feel oppressed, sinned against, misjudged, out of place, and lost. It is a time when we number more enemies than we have and find fault with every friend. On such a day, it is difficult to know why we ever thought life easy.

Faith is much the same. Faith is something which may or may not occur in the process of living. If it occurs, it becomes so much one with life that, like life, it is subject to rhythms of darkness and light, near despair and transcendent joy.

Nothing is more sensitively attuned to the mystery of faith than human life. The sacredness of human life is the most accessible common denominator between men of faith and men of no faith. Whether men believe in God or not, human life emerges as the first and last of those realities in which men have faith. A man of faith believes in life as he believes in God. He discovers God because he finds himself alive and, believing in life, he believes it will not end. His heart cries out for God because of its hunger for life. In this way, he attains God who rejects no man who loves life profoundly even though he may not have known that the core and center of the life he loved was a Love so vital that death had no hold over it and hatred no ability to restrain it.

Every man turns to faith. Those who believe in God believe in him because they are aware that life must never be in vain and that, without God, this could happen. Faith is a man's way of declaring that the life in which all men of good will believe in is worthy of more faith than most men imagine.

1
THERE IS A TIME FOR GIVING BIRTH

A God who creates is a God who has made a commitment to life. God is therefore never indifferent to life. The God we worship is a life-giving God. In celebrating life, we encounter God; in worshipping God we celebrate life. For God *is* Life.

God has made a commitment to human life. This commitment to life, to us, is the heart of the Christian doctrine of divine Providence. Some, as Deists, for example, maintain that the Giver of life allows the life he gives to go its way unsupported.

But Christian doctrine professes that neither God nor man is trustworthy if he gives life and then fails to exercise concern for life. Fatherhood, divine or human, is the difference between begetting life and fostering life.

Something of God was given to man in the mystery of life. As we give physical or spiritual life to others only at the expenditure of ourselves, so God expends himself that others might live. It is not possible to say that a child is the image of its parent unless the parent has so identified himself with the child that one is the image of the other. If man is made in the image of God, it is because God has identified himself with man in some way.

But what does it mean to be born? To be born is to receive a gift. To be born is to be given a promise. Christianity believes that the life-giving God whom we worship is a gift-giving God whose gift is life. Human life has its origins in Life itself. And life allows life to happen as a gift. All of a sudden, one is born, alive; he is; and although he did not request or expect life, everything in him craves life, clings to life, fights for life, keeps life. It is as though there is a universal awareness, at least in the beginning, that to be born is to be gifted and that the gift of birth must be preserved.

Life is the common denominator all men share in the search for God. This God is alive not only in himself but in the life of every man. The God of life is a creating God, a God who makes human life not merely the object of his love but a partner in his love. A God who creates life is glorified and expressed in life; he is dishonored in every refusal or denial of life. A God who

allows birth to happen is a God who orients all creation to life; he beholds in life the fulfillment and finality of creative process.

Every age seeks some way to express the human instinct for reverence and the human heart's sensitivity to something sacred in reality. Human life mediates the sacred to our age more persuasively than any other experience. The wonder of life, its capacity for faith, its essential elusiveness, its intriguing incompleteness, its unwillingness to die tell men that life is a force not to be secularized.

Life irrepressibly seeks more life, different life, other life. Life becomes a desperate experience only when it is denied, contained, misrouted, discounted. Life proves its own redeemer when men allow life to take them beyond the limited horizons we impose upon it into that world of Mystery and Wonder which is life's true home and its sole salvation. Life is a quest which resists our efforts to set it at rest or to allow it to take any path at all. Life needs direction for its tranquility, discovery for its integration. Unless life is properly situated its direction becomes hapless, its discovery chaotic and confused.

Man, a creature of this earth, has been made in the image of God who is committed to this planet without being bound by it and who engendered life on this earth even though this need not have come to pass. Man is earth-bound and God-destined simultaneously. This accounts for his inability to find a home on the other planets unless he makes them similar to his former home. It explains why the only home for which man can become completely homeless is God.

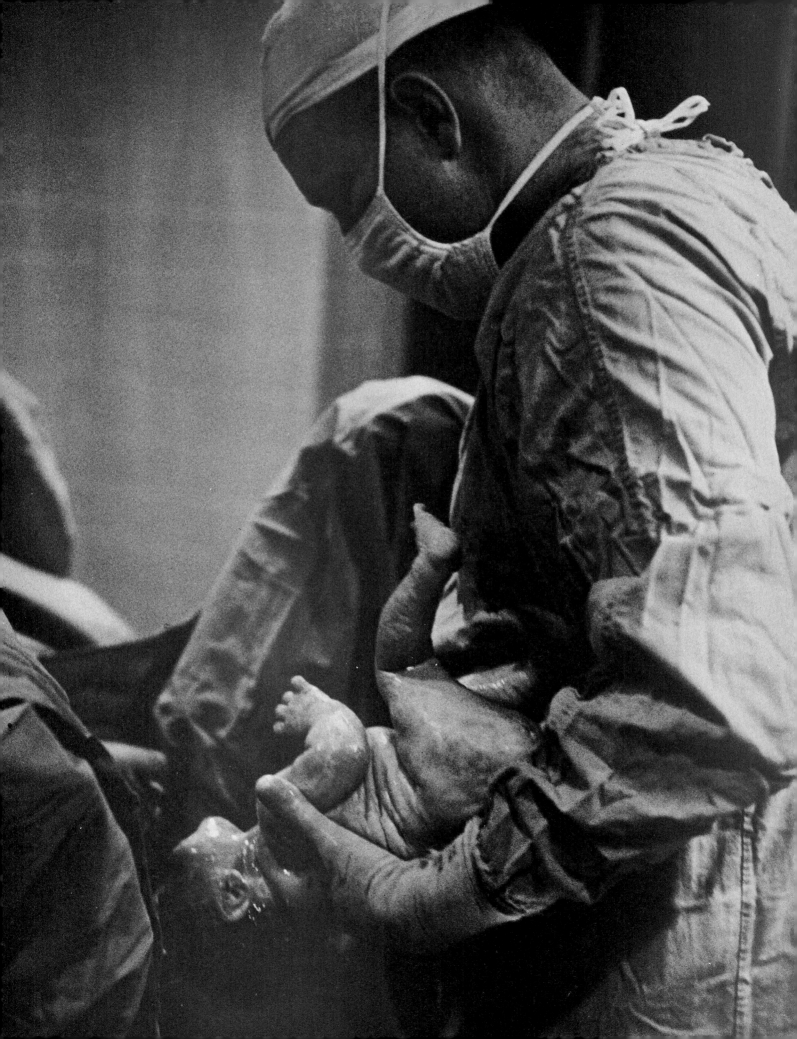

Consciousness

The miracle of life depends upon awareness. Had God been a Force unaware of his intent, undetermined by any goal, ignorant of the consequences of his own action, life would have been matter's finest moment but it would have been neither grace nor gift. Life would have been a perishable accident of nature with no inner harmony; it would have been a reality more sensitive to its chemical origins and its eventual extinction than to its possibilities for further life. Had life occurred in unawareness, God might have been a cosmological wonder-worker but he would not have found himself in his creation nor would his creation discover itself as it wondered about him.

When we Christians confess the Trinity we refer to a God who was aware of himself and, in each Person, aware of something other than himself. God is a God who says forever "I am" only because he can also say to himself "You are." For someone to say of God "He is," something outside of God and yet within his mystery had to be made aware. God objectified himself by creating subjects. In the creation of reflexively conscious subjects, God's "I am" declaration took on further meaning. Now "You are" had reference to divine Sonship but also to an Incarnate God, to Jesus the Christ, and to his many brethren. Unless man was made aware of what God had done to and for him, God would have remained a God who made wonderful things by his power but a God who found neither freedom nor intelligent awareness outside the divine.

God made man aware. Thus, the creating God is a God who creates awareness. The Incarnation intensifies this awareness by revealing to us further experience into the nature of God and of man.

The beginnings of man were indeed sacred. For in these beginnings, Awareness becomes aware in a new way and Life lives differently. In the beginnings of man, God becomes Father by a new definition and Sonship involves not only a divine Person, but other persons. In the beginning of man, a new God was at issue, a creating God, a God who now gives life to that which was less than divine, a God who would be glorified by created freedom and discovered by limited intelligence. Love took on a new form in the creation of man and man found that he too could say "I am" because he was able to realize "You are."

Man found that, sacred though he is, his "I am" could not say as much as God's "I am" and his "You are" was not satisfied by his brothers and sisters. Man, this sacred creature whose sacredness was almost impossible to exaggerate, had a capacity for someone more sacred than himself.

If man's beginnings were sacred, there is reason to believe his destiny would also be significant. A creature of the earth, of a chance planet it seemed, emerged with an infinite hunger for life. This creature wondered about that silent "You are" beyond all the planets and the stars who made him aware of his "I am" and left him unfinished. It was good to be alive, but what if alive-ness reached the life of God and touched upon pure Life?

The time for giving birth is also a time for making a promise. And God who gave birth to man in the dust of the earth and beneath the stars of heaven made man a promise. A time for giving birth is made sacred when it includes a promise that this life given at birth will not be all there is to life.

2
THERE IS A TIME FOR KEEPING

As life goes its way, each man discovers some things which he treasures. Of all the realities man has come upon in his historical pilgrimage, no reality has been deemed more worth preserving than life. Unfortunately, men often know they should preserve values which they do not preserve in fact. Sometimes they even limit their definition of the life which should be preserved to a circle of friends or countrymen.

But life is for keeping. And men know that a man of good will is a man who believes this. Life has been given for a purpose. Its purpose, however, cannot be realized unless every effort is made to preserve the life of every man in every way possible. The preservation of life intends its qualitative enrichment rather than its statistical increment. Since we are incarnational creatures, however, the neglect of life, even biologically, weakens our defense of life qualitatively and spiritually.

Life is for keeping just as promises are for keeping. One gives a promise because he is confident he can fulfill it and because he wants another to trust him. Life was given by God who fulfills life when those who have life trust him as he wishes. God is confident that life is fulfilling; he wants us to trust him to fulfill it.

If life is not for keeping, then the Promise at the heart of all promise is unreliable. If life is not for keeping, then promises have been broken. To believe life leads nowhere is to disbelieve all promises. To believe life has a measured meaning but no infinite meaning is to believe that promises are at best half-hearted. To believe life leads Everywhere and reaches Everyone is to trust in limitless promises.

To destroy life is to break a promise. To disbelieve life is to believe in deception and illusion. For, life invites confidence. And if the confidence it invites ends in death, then confidence is eventually pointless.

No reality challenges trust more or invites confidence so frequently as does life. If life can be annihilated, then all promises are less solemn, less sacred, less secure than we imagined. If life is not for keeping, then promises are not for keeping. If life is taken away, then confidence goes with it. If life invites us to what must one

day be nothing, then promises are for trivial things and for transitory values. If life can one day become dust and nothing more, then promises will one day be words and little else.

Life is always something which happens between two persons. It may occur between God and myself. Or it may begin between a lover and the beloved. Or it may arise between friend and friend. But life, physical or spiritual, always happens between two people. Like promises, life requires someone to pledge faithfulness to and someone to receive one's pledge of fidelity. When life occurs between God and myself, God promises to be faithful to me; in his pledge of fidelity I receive fidelity and return fidelity. When life begins between a lover and the beloved, a promise is made so deep and strong, so pure and lasting that another human being enters history. When life arises between friend and friend, it is because each saw in the other's life a promise he did not have or could not offer but which together they made possible.

Every promise is life-giving just as life is always promise-filled. Life and promise—they are inseparable.

Life is preserved, truly for keeping, when men are faithful to life. Promises are kept, truly honored, when men are faithful to their word. All human fidelity is ultimately fidelity to life. But how is life preserved?

Life is preserved when men are faithful to themselves, to others, and to life's Source. Faithfulness to self requires that one sense his own being, that he appreciate his own aliveness, and that he follow himself to the ends of his own identity and beyond that into the deeper Identity beyond him. It is a perilous journey and many hesitate to undertake it. The easier way is faithfulness to a system, faithfulness to a structure, faithfulness to achievements, faithfulness to success. It is an easier way but it is often purchased at the price of infidelity to self. Men declare God dead or dismiss him because they have been unfaithful to themselves, fearful of where life may lead them, and, therefore, unable to rely on life's Perfection.

The rejection of God can, of course, be a rejection of the artificial God believers put in place of God when they too fear life. More often, however, the rejection of God is a man's final step in the refusal of life. Such a man becomes immersed in life's tasks or life's possessions rather than in life itself. God seems unimportant because a man has lost himself, his experience of what it means to be alive, his awareness of his own identity. When he senses himself no more, he no longer senses God. For God reveals himself to the heart of man. And when man loses his heart, he has lost that which senses God most acutely.

When men are faithful to their own lives, they preserve the lives of others. Man was never made to be given to objects. He was made by Life for Life. He never serves anything else well. The cultural crisis and the faith crisis we face is really a life crisis—a crisis which has come upon us because as a people or as a Christian community we were in danger of forsaking life. This is why we have so little reason for fear. Men are saying today that they are starved for life and surfeited with lifeless realities. Men are reaching for life and since there is no other way to more life, they are reaching for God. The Spirit of God has made us restless for life; we can resist what is happening to us today, in our hearts and souls, in our bones and blood, only at the peril of resisting Life. The moment we are living through is a moment meant to remind us that we were not created for death or for comfort, for objects or for structures, for rigidity or for stability. We were created for Life and life must of its very nature resist death, reject comfort, turn from objects, look beyond structures, shatter rigidity and tire of stability.

Faithfulness to life's Source begins with faithfulness to self and ends there. A man of faith can say this because faithfulness to self presupposes and demands total fidelity, fidelity even to the One who made the self each one discovers and made each self an image of himself. No one faithful to self, in this way, loses God. God is lost because we lose touch with ourselves, remain only on the surface of ourselves, or turn in fear from ourselves to lesser values. God awaits the man who is patient with himself; encounters the man who does not fear himself; redeems the man who accepts himself in courage and grace because he does not fear the demands of life which become the demands of others because they are the demands of God.

Infidelity, then, is ultimately infidelity to life. This is one reason why human history requires a people structured as a community to stand for life and to represent nothing else. Men must be encouraged to believe in life because we are constantly tempted to lose faith in it; we must be reminded of life's sacredness because we continually seek to make it secular and to keep ourselves insulated from God who demands life and who has only life to offer.

Infidelity to life can occur in dramatic ways when, for example, we destroy someone's life, sinning against the sanctity of the other and the holiness of life. It is present when we end our own lives, resisting the demands of life, terminating abruptly our awareness of ourselves, treating as expendable a value which was meant to be absolute and ultimate. These are instances of dramatic infidelity.

There are, however, more subtle ways in which we become unfaithful to life. We do not meet life's demands when we refuse to permit developing life to complete its course or when we hasten the end of life by taking positive steps against it when life can yet support itself. In the one case, a person is not allowed to assert his identity but dies as an embryo or a fetus; in the other case, an identity already established is removed because we decide that pain is more imperative than life.

Most subtle of all is the infidelity to life which occurs when that act from which alone life can issue is frustrated in terms of its ultimate finality. Men of good will differ sharply on this moral issue. It is not unreasonable, however, to maintain that an act which is love's most intensive physical expression and life's only means to birth should not be performed artificially.

In any case, man loses nothing when he is faithful to life, even though this is at times an arduous fidelity. He loses everything when he is unfaithful to life. For, when man is unfaithful to life, his fidelity to everything else is in peril.

3
THERE IS A TIME FOR SPEAKING

The life of man differs from the life of all else on the planet because only the life of man has a history to it. History, precisely defined, only happens when persons are at issue. History requires a memory for the past and freedom for the future. Only man remembers or hopes. Only man recalls his origins and considers his destiny. We have a record of less than human life on this planet but we have no history of it. Even the record of this life cannot be maintained by itself but must be kept by historical man.

It is a distinctive feature of human life that it lives in continuity. This means that man recognizes himself in the history of his ancestors whom he never met; it means that man is aware that those future men he shall never know depend upon what he becomes today for what they will become tomorrow.

Life which is less than human repeats itself, dies out, re-emerges, or evolves. Its main thrust is survival. If it survives, even in an evolutive form, it has achieved its purpose. There is no collective wisdom, no growth in freedom, no concern for meaning, no vision of the future in such life. Thus, there is no history, no continuity properly so called, nothing to pass down, and nothing to strive toward consciously.

Continuity is a crucial element in human living. Something of what we are today is linked with our past. Those things which accounted for our beginnings and occurred in our development affect the way we define ourselves, how we handle our freedom, who we are, and why we are what we are. This past includes creation, an original sin, a turbulent and glorious struggle for life. This past remembers caves and wars, palaces and kings, ships and chariots. It includes paintings on stones and pyramids, the temple of Solomon and the Acropolis, the American Indian and the African Negro. Every piece in the picture is a piece of ourselves. This is not rhetoric, but a profound metaphysical truth.

Though we do not advert to it often, hope depends not only upon our attitude toward the future but upon our memory of the past. Our hope is established in more than our present resources and our distant dreams. It derives from

the fact that we have prevailed. We have mastered the planet and humanized it. We have taken into our control evolution and the environment. We have even ventured to the surface of other celestial bodies not naturally meant for man and yet enriched because man came to them.

It is the memory of where we have been and what we withstood which inspires courage and makes hope sturdy. In his thoughtful play, *The Skin of Our Teeth,* Thornton Wilder has Mr. Antrobus, the symbol of man, remind us of how our future is linked with our past:

. . . my books! They haven't been lost, have they? . . . we almost lost them once before. And when we finally did collect a few torn copies out of old cellars they ran in everyone's head like a fever. They as good as rebuilt the world . . . Oh, I've never forgotten for long at a time that living is struggle. I know that every good and excellent thing in the world stands moment by moment on the razor-edge of danger and must be fought for—whether it's a field, or a home, or a country. All I ask is the chance to build new worlds and God has always given us that. And has given us . . . voices to guide us; and the memory of our mistakes to warn us . . . I will remember in peacetime all the resolves that were so close to us in the days of war. We've come a long ways. We've learned. We're learning. And the steps of our journey are marked for us . . . in these books.

Every parent tells the story of his own life to his children, the history of the family, and the manner in which the lives of relatives and friends were lived. A child is eager for the story of the past because he senses in a way adults sometimes forget that what happened before he was born or before he could remember is necessary for his self-understanding. A parent serves his child best when he tells the story precisely and when he transmits not only the facts but the values behind the facts.

It may not always be necessary for a child to know that his ancestors built a cathedral. More important than the stained glass and the graceful spires or the year when the building was completed is that which men sought to say when they did this. A child can be shown a cathedral but he will never know what a cathedral is unless he knows that the heart of man is anxious for God. More significant than Chartres is the force of a faith which could build Chartres and York, Notre Dame and St. Peter's.

It is important that a child know we once lived in caves but more crucial is an appreciation of why we left them. We left the caves for the same reason why we left this planet. Something is missing. We explored the cave and knowing we needed something more, we left the cave. When we mastered the earth, we wondered if the someone or something more we needed was on the moon or on Mars or, perhaps, beyond them.

There are three billion of us who have learned a million different words in more languages than any one man can learn. And yet we have difficulty communicating and we are often lonely. We have sought and remembered one another, been kind to one another and even died for one another. We have hoped in one another and even at times despaired of one another. We have had faith in our future and love so ardent that it broke our hearts at times. We have done all this and yet something is missing. Something or someone beyond every horizon and more inaccessible than the stars keeps telling us "not yet", "there is more", "this planet is not home nor this love your final love". Someone makes us realize that we wish further life. In the death of each of our beloved fellow-men we realize that no one of us can satisfy this longing for life. Something is not yet right, we know, every time a human being dies and we can have him no longer. This cannot be the way it was meant to be. This cannot be all there is.

Life lives for continuity and in continuity. There is a time when men must speak of this.

No life is lived in isolation. All life occurs in relationships. Even the life of God is the life of Someone who found other Persons when he expressed himself.

Life begins in relationships with others, in continuity with the past and care for the future. Every man who tries to live absolutely, without others, tries to do what even God cannot do. The Father understands himself because there is a

Son and a Spirit. Only Satan seeks to isolate himself. For, hell is no more than the breaking of all the bonds by which each life might have discovered something more than its own existence.

There is a time for speaking, a time to offer one another words of memory and hope, a time to tell about our brothers who left the caves and our sons who shall reach the outer planets. There is a time for speaking when men must proclaim the God from whom we had our beginning, a time when we must confess the grace which kept us from failing so decisively that we could no longer be saved.

Human life, as we know, must begin. Even before life begins (when one considers the act of love from which life can occur) and most certainly after life has begun to be, life must be preserved. Its preservation requires not only fidelity to life as it is, which we considered in our last chapter, but the memory of life as it was. The future of life is inseparable from the reverence with which we honor the life we have and from the history of life as it goes its way in hope.

We need to know not only our dreams but the dreams of our fathers and mothers. We must realize not only our hopes but also the hopes of our history; we share in an enterprise which began in hope and which reached us because there was always more hope in the human heart than circumstances justified. We must achieve the past as well as attain the horizons of the future because our heart is estranged until it becomes familiar with the fraternity and friendship, the love and courage which beat in other hearts before they came to life in our own.

It is especially difficult to ascertain what it may have been in our history which was more pivotal than anything else. A man of faith believes that faith is central. We mentioned before that the mystery of life is bound up with promises. The deepest promise life offers is the promise of God. This is the Promise which invites us to affirm that life is forever and its meaning infinite. This is the Promise which assures us that every human life is divine in some way.

Faith is not only God's gift to us but also our

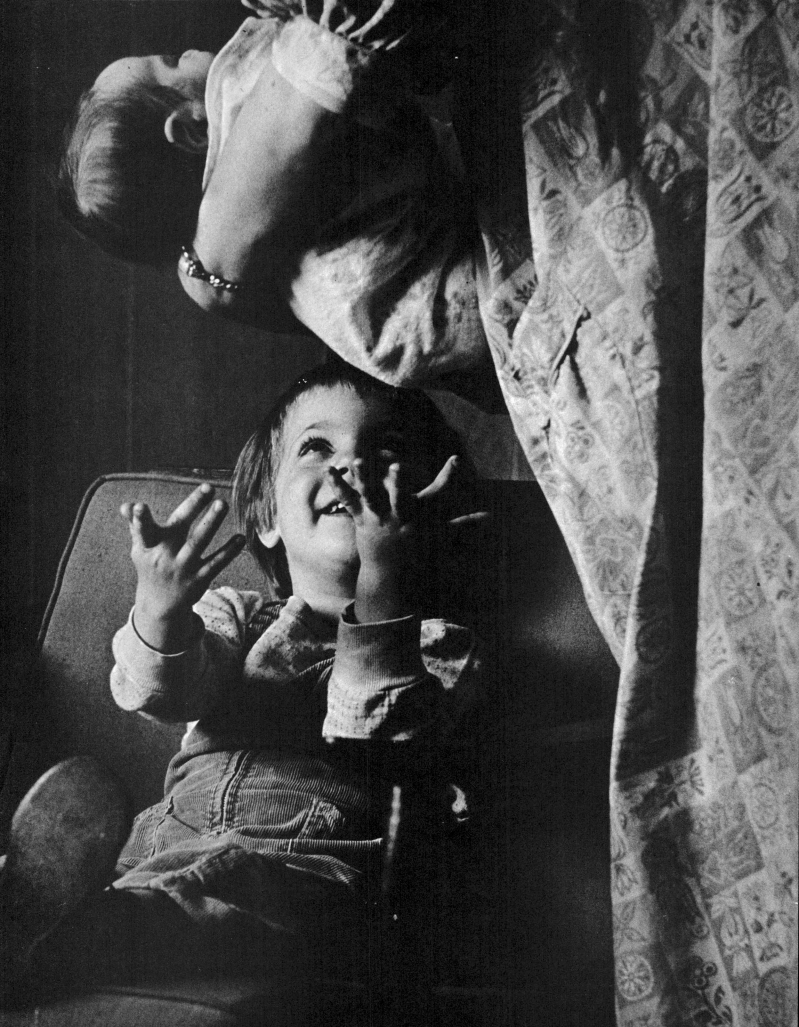

gift to one another. Like life, faith lives in continuity. Like life, faith is handed down. And, like life, faith is both human and divine. Life's promises are redeemed when men speak to one another the fullest meaning of life as they understand it in the context of love. This fullest meaning embraces God and the supernatural order. It is a meaning offered in grace by those who become sacraments of faith for those to whom they witness God. When a father or a mother tells a child that life is ultimately about God and that life always leads to Life, they transmit to someone they love the promises of life and by so doing help engender faith in the heart of a child whose life they physically engendered. When a parent shows by his deeds that the faith he accepts leads to actions inspired by God and that these actions express faith itself, a child beholds the meaning and mystery of life in someone he loves deeply.

Faith, like life, is a process of continuity. It keeps happening because it is handed down as well as given from above. Faith often comes to a child because someone he loved was present with faith before the child was born and because someone the child loved, loved him in the context of faith.

Faith, like life, is relational. We believe because there is a community of believers with whose belief we become identified, even if not always explicitly. Likewise, we live because there is a community of life, the human family, with whose life we become identified, even though at times we may think we are living alone. Life comes from God but it depends upon men who give this life in conditions they must create; it depends upon men to whom we must turn for assistance in living the gift of life we were given.

Faith comes from God but it is related to men who already have faith, men who may have helped faith come to life because of the condi-

tions they created, men to whom we turn when we find we wish to understand better the gift of faith we were given. Faith relates us to God but it also relates us to one another so that we become not only believers in God whose Life we share but also fellow believers in a community of faith whose life we share.

This community has a past which it cherishes and a future it awaits. It communicates not only faith in the present but faith in the past, its tradition, and its sanctifying wisdom. And yet it celebrates faith in the future, its outcome, and its transcendent hope. This community expresses its faith in God by fidelity to its past, commitment to its present, and eagerness for its future. It does this because it knows that the act of faith must embrace all history in confessing the Lord of history. It realizes that God is fully met when men witness to what God has done and to what he is doing and to what he will do.

Faith, like life, has a history. It remembers God and it expects God. It discovers God by recalling him and by waiting for him. Faith is, therefore, a relational reality. It relates us to God and to man. It is grace and sacrament, divine and human, contingent and boundless.

Faith lives in continuity. It is given us by God who chooses to express himself in the words and deeds of our fellowmen, often our parents, sometimes our friends, more ultimately the community of faith, most finally in Christ. When men tell men life is all promise, they are speaking of faith though they may call it something else. When men are aware that God redeemed his promises in the past and continues to promise in the present that which will be fulfilled in the future, they have made an act of faith.

There is a time, then, for speaking about life and about faith. Unless such a time comes, men miss the mystery of life and the majesty of faith. There is a time for speaking, a time when men ought not be silent. When that which men speak concerns the promises of life and affects faith, their words are sacramental and healing signs, instruments by which grace is imparted and life intensified. In such moments, there is no time for silence. It is a time for speaking so that life may continue and faith live.

4
THERE IS A TIME FOR LOVING

There is, as we know, a time for giving birth, a time for fidelity to life and the preservation of it, a time for speaking that life may continue with values and wisdom, with insight and faith. There is a time when no compromise is permissible, a time when belief must be expressed, and promises pledged. There is a time when there is no time for death or for doubt, for despair or disillusionment. There is a time when only birth is proper, hope fitting, words suitable, faith adequate.

Life is an absolute value since it never cedes to death in the Christian interpretation of reality; it is merely transformed into further life. Life exists, as we have said frequently, in relationship. Even as an absolute value, life is in relationship with love, which is the only other absolute value. Life is for love and love leads to life. The contemporary conviction that life and love are absolute values is unmistakably accurate. Of these values, love is ultimate since there are times when even life may be sacrificed on its behalf. But love is the only value for which life may be given.

Love can occur provided that life is present. And love returns the favor, as it were, since love is always life-giving whether one considers a sexual act of love or a fraternal action of human brotherhood. The man who has no love misuses celibacy and distorts marriage. Every genuine human experience leads to life, physical or spiritual life, often both together.

A man who has turned aside from love as the ultimate value dissipates himself by absolutizing less than absolute values. An absolute value is one which contains in itself its own intelligibility and which enters into the essential definition of ultimate value. Thus life has in itself its own meaning; and, it is essential to love. There is no life without love and no love without life. Jesus was able to say that he had come so that we might have life and have it more abundantly. But in doing this, he had to oblige us to love as his only commandment. When men accept the saying of Jesus, "I am life", they begin to understand that further New Testament proclamation, "God is love".

The question, often raised today, concerning situation ethics is not really a question about whether or not love is ultimate. No Christian can rightfully disagree with this assertion, especially since he defines God as love at the same time as he accepts God as the absolute Absolute. There is, however, some question as to how one defines love and whether an individual needs a community to assist him in the formulation of the definition.

The more fundamental ethical or moral question is not the one which asks whether love is ultimate (it is) nor whether the individual must at times decide for himself how love is to be realized in this concrete situation not precisely defined by a community (he must). The question is whether it is possible for a community to define love more effectively than the individual can so that a reliable standard emerges, a standard assuring the personal enrichment of the individual and his growth in love although he may feel quite the opposite at the moment when a choice must be made.

A Christian is someone who knows that moral norms must not be the primary concern of the community to which he pertains. Moral norms are the accidental, oblique, and secondary phenomena which are developed so that the faith identity of the believer may be preserved. By this we mean that faith in Christ should lead one to behave in a certain way.

Faith in Love and acceptance of the commandment of love require certain actions and attitudes on our part. One cannot, for example, say that he believes in human life when he is casual about its preservation, unconcerned about social justice for the starving, eager for war as an instrument of international diplomacy or national prestige. Such actions undermine belief in human life so that sooner or later there is less belief.

One might suggest, more controversially, that a firm belief in human life would seem to make one resistant to abortion and unwilling to consider artificial birth control as the best solution to the problem and promise of marital love. To destroy life already begun in the womb or to frustrate an act which can create life if it is not interfered with seem to go counter to belief in human life. One cannot judge the moral guilt or subjective dispositions of people who so decide but he can evaluate the over-all problem and its objective consistency with faith in life.

In any case, the point we now consider is the question of love. Jesus reveals to us that God is love; he commands us to love as completely as possible and to do this as he did it. Such a vocation is an exciting venture; such a commandment is freedom and grace; such a God is a saving God whose Presence counteracts our lovelessness.

Friendship

There is a time for loving when friendships are formed. This is an experience crucial to love's expression. Friendship is especially important because man has never seemed less alone than in our era. Friendship is also a vital religious value because our age perceives the sacred, as we said, in human relationships rather than in the objective order.

Modern man is deprived of dialogue and personal, spiritual communication more than men were in the past. Together with a more vivid psychological awareness of ourselves there has come about a greater fear of ourselves. With the demise of structured living, the problem of identity and of belonging have been intensified. As the options we are given reach astronomical proportions, the need to converse about them has grown. In the past, human life was put into perspective more easily because of the limitations under which men lived. In the present, when there are fewer limitations, friendship helps us balance our lives more evenly. In a success-oriented culture, friendship is needed to remind us that persons matter more than products.

Friendship is the only reality which dissolves loneliness. It is also vital in the development of faith. Friendship enables us to appreciate faith more fully because, like faith, it is an intensely personal and trans-intellectual experience. Friendship is similar to faith because each of these leads us to discover a partner for dialogue and communion. In friendship, our life is shared

and shared freely. Friendship occurs less in the area of option than anything else we have dealt with thus far in our consideration on life.

Friendship is not the same as participation in a common cause or as that comradeship which derives from the necessity of association. Friendship is present when one person accepts another for what he is and when he knows that he can be more himself with this person than he can be without him. Friendship sometimes brings men together as persons even though their ideologies keep them apart.

Friendship, like faith, has less logic to it than it has personal intuition in its right-ness. No one proves faith to another any more than one can achieve friendship with rules. Friendship and faith are not only known to be right; they are felt to be right. When Christ asked Peter about whether he would leave, Peter answered not with reason but with intuitive knowledge: "If you are wrong, nothing is right. If we lose you, to whom shall we go?"

There is a free-ness about friendship which is even greater than that experienced in marriage. There is less a sense of this having been ordained, less an acceptance of obligation, less urgency in friendship than in marriage. Friendship is so universal an experience that it can occur at every age of man's life. Marriage is something for which one can be too young or too old; friendship is ageless.

Friendship is an experience which touches the lives of those who are married, those who are single, those who are celibate. A married man can be himself with a friend in a way which differs from his being himself with his wife or children. A single girl reveals something of her inner nature to a friend which she may not be able to share with a relative. A person consecrated in celibacy needs friendship for his self-expression and for the development of his spiritual life.

Friendship is a vital and necessary experience. Hardly a person lives who has not known friendship some time in his life; no one lives who cannot be more himself if friendship should happen to him.

Marriage

While friendship means so much, it is marriage which is a sacrament and marriage which witnesses to the unique, exclusive, and life-long love Christ had for his Church. There is something wholly unique and altogether extraordinary about marriage. It is because of marriage that motherhood and fatherhood are holy words; it is because of marriage that the Church can be called a family; it is because of marriage that "home" is the word men cherish more than any other.

There is a time for loving on many levels because marital love happens on one of those levels. Marital love is the only love which creates new life properly; and new life develops best and appreciates love most profoundly in a marital situation.

Christianity depends upon the family for its religious vocabulary more completely than does any other religion. God is presented as Father and Son; Jesus is born of Mary and Joseph; baptism is re-birth; marriage is a symbol of the Church; and the Eucharist makes brothers and sisters of all believers who sacramentally live by the same flesh and blood.

Marriage for a Christian is a vocation rather than a contract, a grace from God rather than a social institution, a revelation of Christ's nature rather than a cultural necessity. The family is "the community wherein Christ is most powerfully preached, where Christians first hear the name of God, first learn to pray, and first express their faith." (*Human Life in Our Day*)

It is in the family that life, faith, and love are concentrated, united, incarnationalized, and transformed. The family is the most effective sign we have of the relationship between life, faith, and love.

The family begins with an act of faith in the sacramental liturgy of the Church. This act of faith is directed not only to God who is Life and Love but to the married partners who believe that from their union life and love will issue in a new way.

And life does come to pass in a new way. Husband and wife live differently in a life neither experienced before marriage. This life, a marital life, has its own expression of love to symbolize the uniqueness of this new life which has come to pass between husband and wife. This life is sustained by the liturgy of the Church whose every sacrament is life-oriented, life-giving, death-resistant.

But new life happens even more dramatically than this in marriage. Husband and wife love each other sexually and spiritually in an act which has the power to create human life even as it deepens marital love. When new life comes from this act of love, husband and wife know they are expressed in this new human being and that in this new person they encounter God whom they never met this way before.

The birth of a child is a religious experience which enables husband and wife, now father and mother, to know how great a mystery their love is and how powerful a grace life is. Husband and wife are transcended and transformed in the birth of a child by life itself. They are never the same again because from them has come someone who never lived before, someone who could not have had life unless they had loved.

Parents have their child baptized into the community of faith while they promise that the life and the faith of this child shall be their responsibility before God and the Church. Life, faith, and love become one unit in a child to whom his parents have given life, witnessed faith, and expressed love.

Without marriage, some aspects of the mystery of Christ would have remained unknown to the Church. Christ transformed marriage by revealing through it the family character of the Church, the Paternity and Sonship of God, the sacred symbolism of sexual love, the sacramental

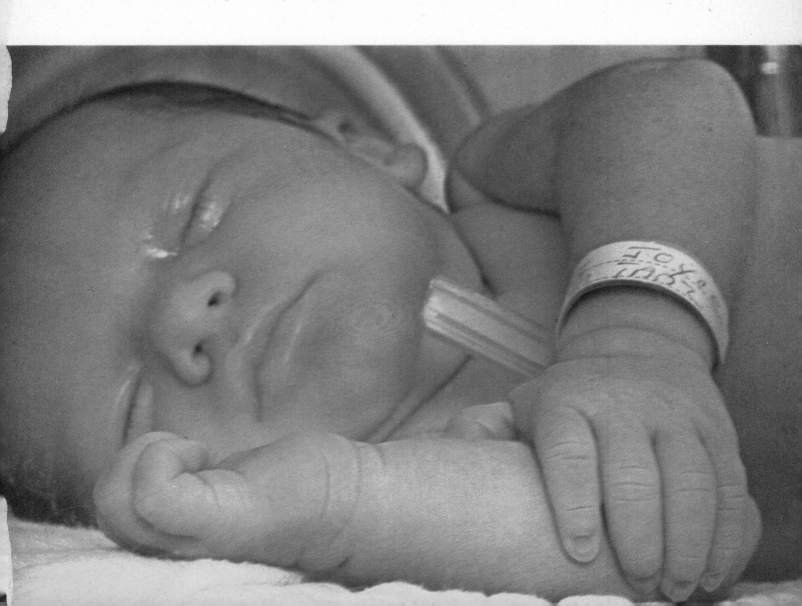

structure of marital life, and the apostolic mission of the Christian home. The Holy Spirit is present to the Church because the Son of God made us aware of the divinity of Fatherhood; this Spirit is with us because the incarnation of God's Son came to pass with the birth of a child who was surrounded by the marital love of Joseph for Mary.

Celibacy

A time for loving means to a Christian something besides friendship and marriage. It includes also the charismatic gift of celibate love.

The most persuasive story of love this world has known occurred in the heart of a Man who was celibate. No love more powerful or more universal ever existed than the love of the celibate Jesus on the cross who became, because of this love, the Christ of Easter glory.

Because of Jesus and his Kingdom, because of grace and the New Testament, the Church can never be the Church of Christ completely unless it makes its members sensitive to the witness of celibate love. There has never been a time in the history of the Church when celibate love was not proposed as an ideal. The Church was yet in the process of apostolic formation when the Scripture was written. And Scripture speaks of a Jesus who did not marry although his culture expected this of him. Scripture includes in its canon the words of St. Paul by which, in the power of the Spirit, he counsels celibate love.

There shall never be a time in the history of the Church when Christians will fail to be impressed by the man or woman who chooses not to marry so that he might express another dimension of love.

Celibacy loses its meaning only when it does not become a way to love; such "celibacy" is more juridical celibacy; it cannot inspire Christians to love Christ and one another; in fact, it often does the reverse.

Christians who accept the gift of celibacy must accept it because there is Christ and because there is love. Someone who is celibate merely to perform a function or, perhaps, to escape the demands of marital love or responsible living, is legally celibate but not charismatically celibate.

Unless there was Christ, Christians would not be as inspired as they are by celibacy. Because there was Christ, they know that a Church which has lost its sensitivity to celibate love has lost Christ in a vital way. A Church which limits its expression of Christian love to marriage is a Church which has lost the fullness of the Spirit's life.

Celibacy makes ultimate sense to a Christian when it is situated in the context of the absoluteness of life and love. Although many who lived in the time of Jesus might have preferred a married Messiah, the New Testament refers to the virginity of Mary and the celibacy of Christ. Although religious Jews saw in marriage an abiding symbol of life and love, Jesus spoke of a type of life and a manner of love offered to those whose radical discipleship caused them to leave husband and wife, children and home.

Celibacy, unlike marriage, is not bound closely to cultural styles of life. It is less institutional, less sacramental than marriage. It is charism, almost pure charism, given to a believing community so that its faith in Christ may be made vital and so that its belief in life and love may never falter.

5
THERE IS A TIME FOR LAUGHTER

There is a time for laughter in life, a time when men sense they are more free than the tragedy or the suffering, the sorrow or the tears which are part of life but not its whole story. Men were made for laughter, for celebration, for the joy which is God and for the freedom which is grace.

There are those who believe that life is torment, a burden to be borne, an absurd situation which has no exit except annihilation. Klaus Mann once summed up the attitude of many modern men, especially in the intellectual community, toward life:

There is no hope. We . . . would do well to recognize our situation as absolutely desperate. Why should we hold false hopes? We are lost! We are defeated! . . . We should abandon ourselves to absolute despair . . .

This is one way to live but it is only one way. It is not *the* way so that a sensitive or intelligent man is compelled to follow this path and no other. There are also persuasive reasons for festivity in the community of men. Life need not be a process of inevitable disillusionment; it is also a discovery of hope for those who choose to discover hope.

One must, of course, recognize the evil which pervades our lives and becomes almost the atmosphere we breathe. The answer to this evil is not always a persuasive theory, a forceful syllogism, or a logical construct. Evil is an experience rather than a concept; salvation from it, therefore, requires a counter-experience rather than a contradictory argument. The most effective response to evil or pain is often, strange as it seems, laughter. Obviously, there are moments when this is not possible because the tears are too bitter or the loss too total to permit anything but grief. There are moments when this is the case but they need only be moments.

It is often said that modern man has lost his sense of sin. I do not believe this is so. Modern man may no longer call his guilt sin but he has not lost his sense of sin. He is more aware than ever before of his alienation and his failure, of the absence of innocence and of the darkness in his heart. He uses different categories to express this but he feels the oppressiveness of

guilt. He does not need a reminder of his perversity or his fragility, of his broken-ness and his crimes. Modern man has lost his sense of humour rather than his sense of sin. He finds it easier to brood about himself than to laugh.

There must be a time for laughter in life or else we are lost. There must be a time when we dance, like Zorba, in the midst of our tragedies and celebrate even our inability to find reasons for celebration.

The very possibility of a time for laughter in our lives tells us something about ourselves. Laughter comes from within the heart of a man. He is able to laugh, even when the objective situation does not demand it, because something in him is not bound by the objective situation. Only men can laugh; an animal has no sense of humour. This is because there is something in man which the heart of an animal cannot contain.

It is possible for us to laugh because we are free. Men have a sense of humour because they have a sense of inner freedom. Nothing can keep a man from laughing, restrain him from celebration, confine him to tears except his inner decision. Men have gone singing to their death and Thomas More, that saint who so intrigues modern man, jested with his executioner.

If modern men have ceased to laugh, if they find humour out of place, it may well be because they no longer believe in their freedom or trust their freedom or love their freedom. It is an unfortunate sign of our times that a man who considers laughter a partial solution to our problems may be judged naive or ill-informed. We have become such strangers to humour and joy that we suspect it; we are tempted to think that the man who laughs must not have felt the pain and sorrow we have felt.

God is more responsible for a sense of humour than anyone else. When men give up on God, they become serious. When they discount faith, they continue to honor reason but they dismiss poetry. When they deride transcendent hope, they emphasize the will rather than the heart of man. Freedom, however, like evil, is something the heart feels before the will makes its choice.

We must not overlook the fact that moral behavior depends upon our sense of life and our doctrine about life more than we realize. The man who believes in goodness is good. The converse is not true. A man who does good things may do them not because he believes in goodness but because he believes in evil so strongly that he scrupulously resists evil with deeds rather than with faith in goodness. A man who truly believes in God turns from evil almost instinctively. His ethics follow upon his faith.

It is grotesque to smile in the midst of life's sorrows if one does not believe there is a point to smiling. One must sense the humour of his heart before he has a sense of humour. He must appreciate the fact that he was not born in sorrow nor lived all his life in sorrow and, therefore, need not believe that sorrow is his natural state or his inevitable outcome.

Faith in God is a man's way of saying there is always something more than sorrow. We said before that giving up on God leads men to turn to intelligence rather than poetry. This is not to say, of course, that intelligence is not essential to life. Sometimes we need clear thinking more than we need anything else. But intelligence without a poetic spirit can make men rationalists. No man ever explained rationally why he fell in love. No Christian will ever demonstrate logically why God created or why his Son died. There is no convincing reason for Easter or Pentecost.

There is a time for laughter because there is poetry in the heart of man and grace and freedom and love and all those other realities no one understands and everyone of us feels. There is a time for laughter because we can have hope even when there are no reasons for it; we can choose life when all circumstances counsel the opposite; we can feel joy in our bones even though everyone around us thinks this foolish. There is a time for laughter because we are always free men; there is a time for laughter because the free God who made us freely for freedom is at the heart of our heart.

We Christians have not spoken enough of the laughter of Jesus. He must have laughed be-cause if ever man was a poet, Jesus was. Jesus spoke of birds in the air and lillies of the field, of seed in the earth and children who played in the market-place. He called God Father and Judas friend.

Jesus was a poet. The things he did had an inner logic which escapes logic and captures the heart. He told us we were God's sons and daughters, that prayer accomplished something, and that peace was his gift to us.

Jesus was a poet who thought the answer to a boat about to sink in the Sea of Galilee was more faith; he thought that a former carpenter from Nazareth was the light of the world and the promised Messiah of God's Kingdom.

Jesus was a poet who spent an evening conversing with a Pharisee about how a man can be born again; one afternoon, he used a drink of water as an occasion to reach a woman's heart with the gift of grace.

Because Jesus was a poet, he must have laughed.

Jesus was the divine poet whose mother was a virgin and who said bread and wine were his body and blood. He was so much a poet that he thought angels could protect him from being captured had he wished; he called himself a king before Pilate and wondered why those who crucified him did not know that he and they were brothers.

There was laughter and joy in the heart of Jesus; there was peace and hope even in the darkness of Calvary and the blackness of the tomb. And God proved himself a poet when he gave his Son human life again on Easter Sunday morning.

There is a time for laughter because there was Jesus who taught us how to dance and to sing, to rejoice and to make Alleluia a prayer. The disciples of Jesus caught the message. Paul spoke of the folly of the cross and Peter baptized the Gentiles although everyone said this was wrong. John said God was light and Matthew remembered how he left his counting-tables to follow the Nazarene.

We are free men whose freedom is trustworthy and whose freedom seeks faith. God is

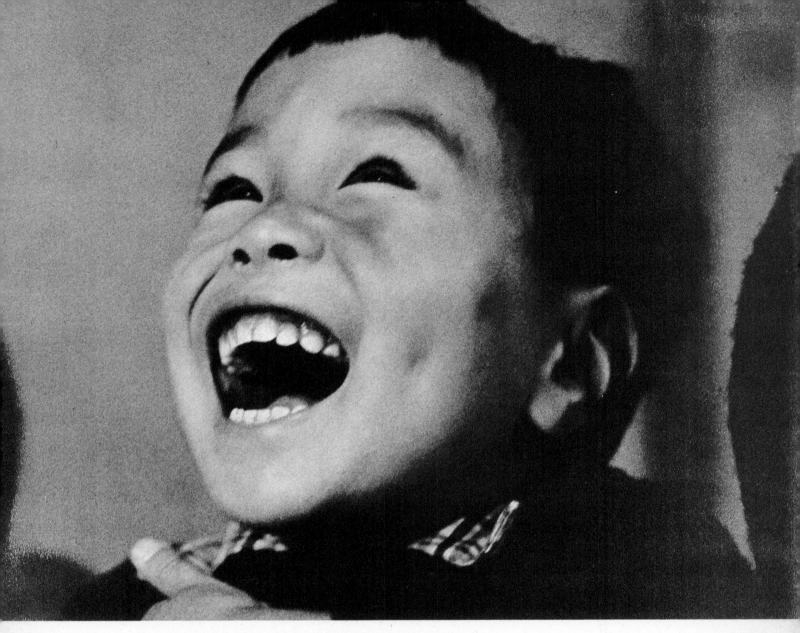

the One who sets us free; from enslavement and sin, from self-preoccupation and somberness. God rescues us from the shores of the Red Sea and from the guilt of having killed his Son, his poet.

We are free men but no one of us feels he is free enough. Somehow every man believes he is entitled to more freedom. The man who does not fear further freedom finds faith. This is the truth which sets men free, a truth which makes faith worthy of freedom. Only in freedom does faith happen. Only for those who wish to be free is faith meant. Only when the heart of man is free can he laugh or worship.

Every one of us has moments when his freedom leads him to laugh. Because there is a time for laughter in every life, there is also a time when men can sense their freedom and affirm faith. Every act of faith is simultaneously an act of freedom or else it is not faith.

There is a time for laughter in life because life is a journey to a land of freedom where, we were promised, God "will wipe away every tear from their eyes, and death shall be no more, neither shall there be mourning nor cry of anguish nor pain any more". (Rev. 20, 4)

Free men have every reason to hope the future is destined for freedom; it provides no objective reason for despair. Our future is a future in which the life faith seeks and the freedom love gives are assured.

Christians are sent ahead to remind men of

this future so that they will not think they are
not free or that they ought not have faith. We
are sent ahead to announce that the land to
which we have not yet come is a land of milk
and honey. This land is worth hoping in; and,
we can laugh about this even if we can laugh
about nothing else.

Christians are sent ahead to tell their brothers
to rejoice and to celebrate life because life has
a wonderful future. Christians must make men
aware that laughter leads to community because, while it is often difficult to cry with a
man, it is always easy to laugh with him.

The Eucharist is the most dramatic sign
Christians use to express their faith and await
man's future, to affirm their hope and assert
man's freedom. This is why, although our Eucharist celebrates the death of Jesus, we sing
and give peace to one another during it.

We know that Jesus must have laughed as
well as wept in his life. Or else why would men
have loved him? Because he laughed and gave
us reasons for laughter, we celebrate the Eucharist as our way of saying that life is to be cele-
brated because our brother Jesus loved us and
saved us and taught us to pray and promised
us that life was joyfully given and would never
be taken away.

6
THERE IS A
TIME FOR
TEARS

Perhaps only the man who has a sense of humour knows what tragedy is. Such a man is acutely aware of the sorrow of life because he has experienced its happiness. He knows that life is tragic in its essence but he is less attuned to tragedy than the man whose vision of life is a vision of darkness. Because he does not consider life to be ultimately absurd, he feels more painfully its absurdities.

There is a time for tears and every man who lives must come to learn this. There is a time when hearts are broken and dreams dispelled. And there is no protection from this, no security secure enough to harbor us from perilous moments or to shield us from the frightening hours of life.

Man, we have been told is not made for safe havens. His life is meant for exposure and risk. The man who expects no failure, resents heartache and turns bitter in grief. He does not accept tears as a revelation to us of what life is and who we are. A man cannot take the measure of himself, perceive his destiny, sense his being or exercise his freedom unless life forces him constantly to summon resources he did not know he had and to prevail in circumstances where he thought only defeat was possible. Unless there is a time for tears, men make a myth of living and expect life to be homecoming rather than pilgrimage. Unless there is a time for tears, men dare nothing. A time when success is assured is a time when men are least successful.

We said before that we laugh because we are free men. We maintain now that we feel tragedy because we must learn that our freedom is limited. A creature's life is never totally at his own disposal. The "only so much", the "not yet", the "just so long" of life leads us to tears. The aching desire to have what we do not have, to be what we are not, to possess what we have lost, to accomplish what is now beyond our reach, brings us to sorrow.

There is a time for tears because we constantly wonder why things might not have been otherwise. Our freedom is at stake in our tears. If we deny our freedom because we suffer in life, we are slaves of our sufferings. At this point,

self-pity replaces responsible freedom. If we refuse to accept the limitations of our freedom, we are foolishly deluded. At this point, we become intoxicated with euphoria and omnipotence.

Tears tell us that we have come to grief because we are free; that we experience sorrow because life is uncertain in all its specifics, that the freedom we possess cannot do for us all we wish to do for ourselves. Karl Jaspers writes that men are conscious of the "more" of life in their experience of their own "less", that they are near transcendence as they verge on collapse.

Christians have a unique insight into the tragedy of life. We believe that even God is not a stranger to tragedy since his Son was rejected in his innocence and crucified while he loved others. God allows his plans to be forestalled, his saints martyred, his Gospel misinterpreted,

his love denied. Even God, it seems, does only so much, goes only so far. He guarantees that life begins and he saves life from total meaninglessness. But he does not preserve us from tears, prevent us from hating him or one another, or free us from the refusal of our own freedoms. God does not abolish death, even for Jesus, nor rescue man from suffering.

Modern man has a tendency to resent suffering in his life, to feel it ought not be there, and to suppose it might have been avoided with proper care. This is false. Men might avoid this or that specific problem, this or that anxiety, this or that malady but he cannot avoid the sense of human life which is inextricably bound up with pain.

Pain is not a by-product or an antecedent, a consequence or an accident of life. It is the very essence of our historical life. This is made known to us in the troubled existence of Jesus and in his tortured death.

Theologians might dispute as to whether life would have been painful without sin or what sin added to the suffering of life. This is, however, another question. The only life we are aware of is the life we have known in our sinful history. Such a life is painful in its essence. To live is to suffer.

The man who meets life with the notion he can avoid suffering or with the conviction that he will rebel against suffering with resentment is a man who misses the essence of life. There is a time when men must shed tears. Even the man who has all the success he can assimilate, all the talent he can manage, all the possessions he can accumulate sheds tears. Even he senses his misplacement. Even he is aware life has not given him enough when it seems to have given him everything. Even he perceives misunderstanding, fears the death of those he loves, and provides for the day when he too must die.

The cross of Christ reveals to mankind the necessity of tears. It tells us beforehand that there will come a time when life will force us to go where we choose not to go. In every man's life, a time comes when there is no exit and when the measure of a man's courage is taken and the depth of his faith and the power of his hope.

There comes a time when men must face life alone, alone on a cross or alone in a prison, alone on a city street or alone in the hours of pain which close out everyone else. There comes a time when a man knows his life can no longer be repaired, a time when he loses in death someone whose loss cuts so sharply that the wound is never healed.

There comes a time when there is only God and only faith in him, nothing else, no one else. Jesus knew this on the cross. A time came when even words could not be spoken, when even the sun became an enemy, and when a cry for help brought vinegar and gall. There comes a time when a man must understand that his life is over and it is time to go.

Life, this profound, sacred, joyful, gracious, divine, peaceful, tender gift is nonetheless vulnerable. Nothing lasts. A friendship we were sure would never end is finished the next day. A marriage, when words like "for better or for worse", "in sickness and in health", "until death–forever" did not seem excessive, is terminated in a few years. Some of our most ardent hopes become, in time, our most bitter memories. Everyone of us remembers an ideal he lost, a promise he did not keep, an expectation he did not live up to.

Tragedy is woven into the fabric of human existence as artfully as grace. Man does not fail because he is inadvertent but because there is

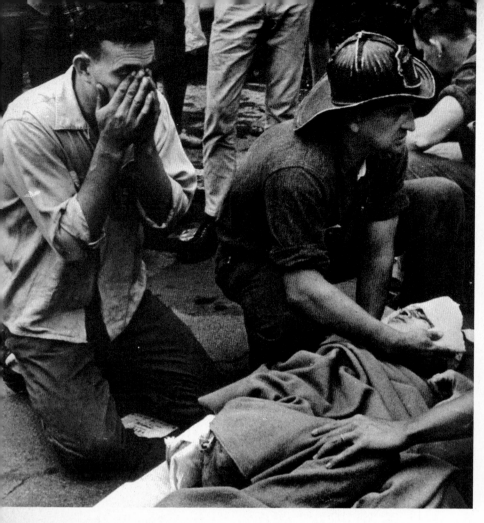

no other way. Jesus is not crucified because he made a mistake but because "it is written".

It is the law of life that life is poured out, wasted, unfinished, disrupted. There is a sense in which every man dies too young and in which no man redeems his promise. We die with more in us than we gave, more in us than others saw, more in us than our friends heard, or our companions noticed. And then suddenly we are dead with so much of our love unexpressed, so many of our lonely hours unrelieved, so many of our happy moments unshared. Too often, no one was there when we were ready to say "I care", "I am happy", "I want to thank you". We die with all this in us, all the times when we tried to say we knew we had made a mistake and then, because the moment passed, could not bring ourselves to say in the next moment that which we almost said a moment ago.

Life is a time for laughter. But there comes a time when the laughter is done and when the confusion or the fear of life catches in our throat. There is a time when the massiveness of what we do not know about life oppresses us and when the magnitude of the venture life is and of the values at stake in living makes us anxious.

There is a time for tears, a time when men have no one to turn to, a time when they do all the right things and yet come to grief. There is a time when life seems God-forsaken and when we feel more acutely the dust of the earth than the breath of God. There is a time when the heavens are dark and the disciples are gone, a time when a few nails and almost unbearable pain are the only remains of a kingdom. There is a time when Easter seems absurd and resurrection impossible, a time when the tomb seems more credible than the Fatherhood of God. There is a time when we are baffled and bewildered and when all we can say is "Father, into your hands . . . Father, into your hands". There is a time when such a time comes. And Christians have no answers at such a time. All they can say is that even God knew a time for tears and that in it he did not despair.

7
THERE IS A TIME FOR BUILDING

It is not always possible to determine whether one is doing something which will eventually prove constructive or where his constructive tasks may be leading him. It is easier to declare that a time for building has come than it is to know exactly what we must build and how to go about it. Like every creative process, building requires giving as well as taking away, putting together as well as taking apart. One must uproot something in order to build.

Society is expected to build community. One of the most critical tools in that building is authority. Authority is meant to be a center of unity for such an endeavor.

We have come upon a time in which we have become less involved with what we build and more concerned with the builder.

A generation or two ago, we were more intensively committed to the projects in hand. There was a Depression to build our way out of, a Second World War to recover from by building a new world from its debris, an international problem with Communism and colonialism to overcome by building free institutions to resist both Soviet and Western enchroachments. It was a time when authority was best exercised in a unilateral fashion. Thus, a strong President, a strong economy, a strong alliance, a strong native leader were needed. When men sense an immediate crisis and devise a short-range goal to meet it, they are less receptive to diversity, dissent, or discussion. Since the First World War, America has been confronted with a series of immediate crises and short-range goals. Monolithic authority was preferred to participatory democracy and its collegial exercise in an atmosphere of national debate.

When the immediate crises are agonizing but not likely to destroy society, we pay more attention to the man who builds than to the building he constructs. Since there is less urgency and clarity about what must be done, we shift our attention to the identity of the builder and the quality of his life.

In such a climate, the first thing we question is the nature of the authority by which we are ruled and the limits of its control over us. Since

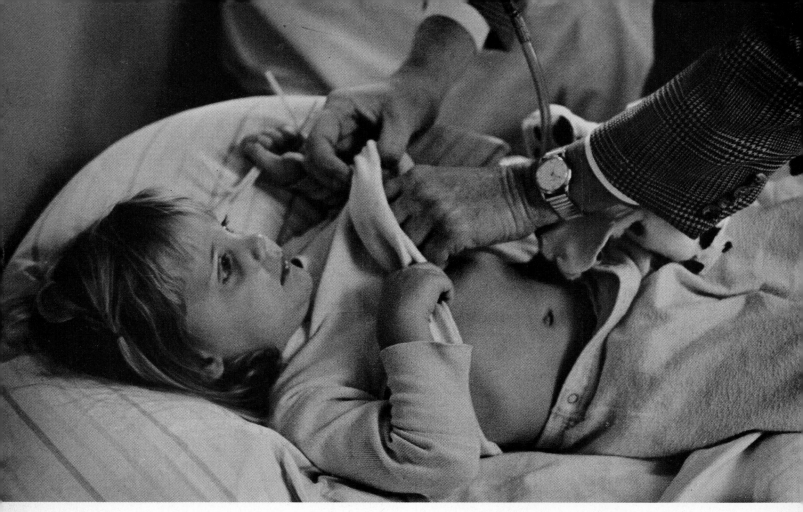

there is no concrete, urgent objective, we emphasize community, participation, personal initiative, and creative alternatives. The pressing need becomes multiformity rather than uniformity. The best guarantee that society is fulfilling its promise becomes the emergence of variety and new forms of living rather than the accomplishment of one single task in a massive national effort. Now tension between those in authority and those whom they represent is not unhealthy. All this would change, our many projects would be abandoned, if another world war or an international depression occurred.

A situation of tension between authority and those whom authority serves is normal. When normalcy is re-asserted, an examination of what authority is can proceed more effectively. The disruption in our national life which we now experience is a reaction, in part, to a prolonged period during which men were forced by the nature of their circumstances to live by more uniformity than normalcy requires.

Authority's authority comes from the need to preserve life and foster love. Authority is not for law and order except as these serve life and love. Authority does not derive its sacred character from its ability to assure social serenity nor from its potential to preserve a particular cultural form nor from its usefulness in maintaining international harmony or economic productivity. Authority's sacred character derives from its relationship with realities which are sacred in themselves, namely life and love. For, law and order can destroy life and foster hatred, as tyranny constantly proves. It is possible to assure social serenity at the expenditure of human values or to perpetuate a particular cultural form for the sake of the few it benefits rather than for the sake of the many who are oppressed by it. There are those who sacrifice the fundamental rights of others for international harmony. And sometimes economic productivity is preserved only if some men are forced to live on a sub-human level or some nations deprived of autonomous identity.

Authority is not sacred except when it allows the sacredness of life and love to assert themselves. Authority must always be on the side of life or else it is no authority. Thus, an authority which sacrifices human life by enforcing artificial birth control or abortion, mass murder or euthanasia is no authority. An authority which decides human rights by color of skin or limits love to ethnic groups or arbitrarily restricts the legitimate options life itself offers is no authority. An authority which wages war for prestige or power or generates an economy which requires slavery or its equivalent for its continuance, an authority which plays politics with human life and human rights is an oppressor to be resisted rather than a sacred institution to be heeded. Authority is worth hearing and worthy of its sacred character when it deems human life so sacred that it is not negotiable and when it fosters human love as the ultimate value by which all other values are to be normed.

The present time is a time for building society and community in a new way. It is a time when we are acutely aware that a principle of unity with no variety is uniformity. Life, however, seeks not uniformity but unity for its enrichment. This is a time when we build by taking new paths rather than by remaining in one place and raising one building together. It is a time when we are asking ourselves whether life need go the way we once thought it must go. We wonder about a wholly different path, another way which, even if it be no better in itself, may be better at least in this that we tried something else. The most creative pioneer venture of the moment will be the one that helps life to happen differently and yet keeps it continuous with the wisdom of the past. Unless we do this our new-ness will not be new-ness because we shall have to undo it at some point in the future.

We are in a stage of transition. We have emerged from a time when commitment to form and institution, to structure and tradition mediated life and were essential to life's survival and life's continuity. We are entering a time when these commitments will stifle life unless they are counter-balanced.

History records moments when life is crys-

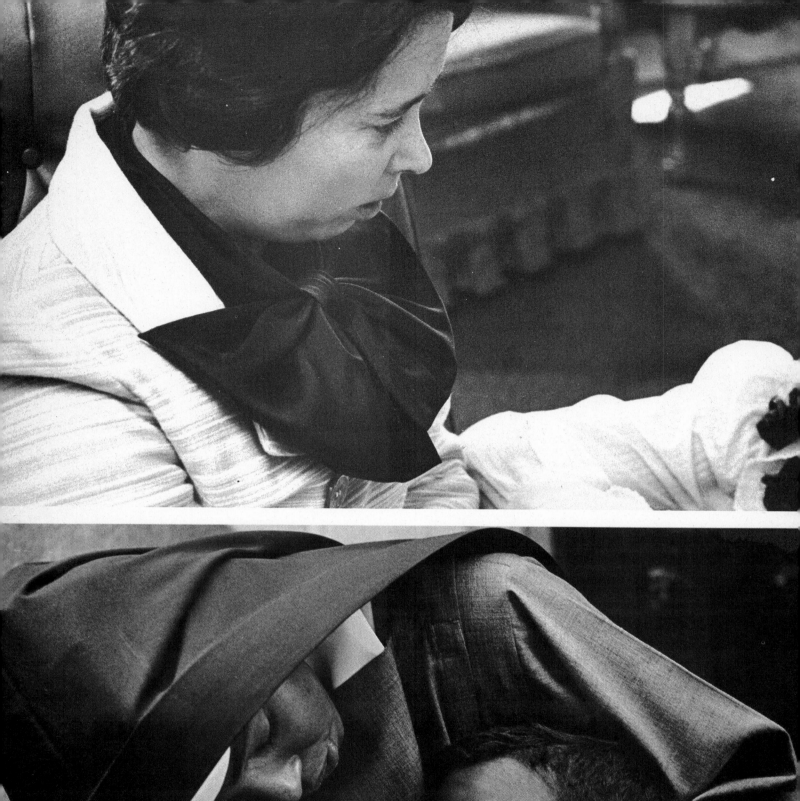

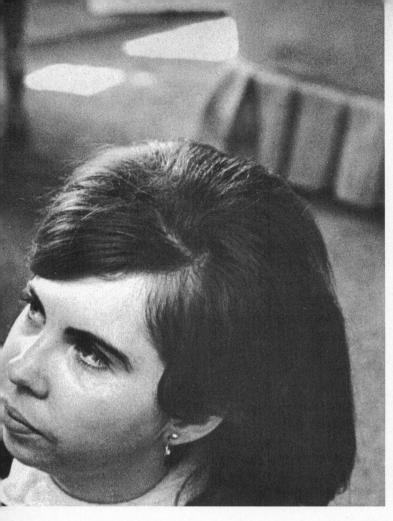

complishments, a sense of one's own being rather than a sense of success. This may require a re-definition of what education is, a re-affirmation of the principle of participation, a re-structuring of society so that the talent of youth can be utilized.

But life and love cannot be served well unless the young generation realizes that every generation is hungry for life and that no generation has a monopoly on idealism or generosity. The same generation now seen as "the Establishment" by young people is the generation which fought wars for freedom, legislated social security, struggled for labor reform, declared "separate but equal" unconstitutional, and tried to give their children opportunities they never had.

Authority will not long survive if it becomes unmindful of life or of love. Life will assert itself against everything which represses it. And authority, since it is exercised by fallible men, will tend sooner or later to be misused. Authority, therefore, should at times be put under pressure. Sanity demands, however, that those who besiege it must realize that the purpose of such pressure is not the abolition but the purification of authority. If authority is destroyed, freedom goes with it. If authority is taken away, life is jeopardized and love threatened. Since the principle behind authority is a force for life, life will constantly seek authority for its refinement and direction, for its unification and ordered expression.

There are many truths we must keep in mind as we assess our present situation. The turmoil we are enduring has come about because something was amiss in the world and in the Church. Men had to recall that the heart of man must be preserved at all costs. Christians had to remember that the Gospel normed the Church and that the Church served life and love or else it compromised its mission.

A time to build in a different way came in our lifetime, a time to build other buildings, find other paths, live other styles of life, love with a new set of categories. A time came when we were asked to build fewer walls and a few more bridges.

tallized and moments when it is unfrozen. The crystallization is useful only if it solidifies pivotal values. The values of two generations ago cannot be crystallized as an answer to the values which are needed today. They were crystallized to serve life then. A generation or two hence that which we are doing today will be crystallized for a while. But a time will come when crystallization will again threaten rather than serve.

The world stays young only if it does not stand still for too long a time. Today the world seeks its youth again. If our finite values are not constantly challenged they will not remain as values; for, then, they pretend to infinity. Finite institutions must be repeatedly reformed or else they imprison rather than serve.

The young generation in America is a reminder to us of our finite-ness. It speaks to a generation that is weary with war of new possibilities for peace. It directs our attention to the primacy of love over stability. It asks us to consider human relationships more than human ac-

8
THERE IS A TIME FOR KEEPING SILENT

Silence, as we define it, is not the same as not talking, nor is it equivalent with the absence of noise. Silence is an inner dialogue, an active conversation which is unverbalized not because one chooses not to speak but because there are no words for what is happening.

A child cannot say why a balloon fills him with joy; a poet cannot find words to match his wonder at the stars or the sea; a musician is at a loss to explain what Beethoven does to him; a man in love cannot express himself adequately.

Silence happens to a person because of what life does to him. There are times when words destroy the interior harmony of a person. The rhythm of human development sometimes needs silence rather than speech.

The wonder of life and the wonder of one's awareness of life make us silent. Silence serves a purpose because there is a mystery to ourselves, a mystery which eludes all our talking to one another, a mystery which envelops us at moments and makes us pause in surprise or contemplation. To talk at such moments is to lose something of ourselves. There are times when words heal and reveal, times when words bring us life, times when our words bring others life. But there is also a time for keeping silent. There are times when words say nothing and when silence expresses everything.

Life cannot be summed up in deeds or comprehended in words. It requires awareness and silence. Life is not something to be done; it is something to be felt; it is given us to make us reverent before its mystery rather than merely as a means to reach goals. Life is its own achievement; it makes us silent so that we shall understand that no accomplishment of man equals the mystery and gift of his own presence. Silence convinces us that life is not what we say it is or make it to be. It is more. There is something divine about life, something we cannot contain, something which bewilders us at moments when we think we have it figured out.

Silence brings us into vital contact with those things in life which cannot be encountered in action but require reflection and tranquility. A child knows this. A child often stops all his activity and looks within himself so that he

might grasp what is happening to him. An adolescent is often wonder-struck or bewildered at the fact that he seems at one moment to have outgrown himself and at another to have grown not quickly enough.

A man who is pragmatic tends to inquire about the concrete results of silence. One can, he reasons, measure the worth of another's words or evaluate the utility of another's deeds. But what can one do pragmatically with silence?

The silence of which we are speaking leads to self-awareness and life-awareness. If, as we said before, there is something divine about human life, if God is at the heart of our hearts, then life-awareness can lead easily to God-awareness. God is dead for men who do not know how to be silent and who, therefore, fail to appreciate the wonder-filled experience of being alive. God is Life and the man who has no care for life has little for God.

It is especially fortunate that we have learned since the Council to pray more effectively in dialogue with one another. This horizontal dimension of our prayer-experience has been an asset. We have learned to pray not only side by side but together. And this is good.

But the dialogical structure of prayer must be expressed not only in the prayer which explicity links us with the charism and charity of others but in the prayer which makes us silently conscious of the Otherness of God. This vertical dimension of our prayer-experience is essential. Sometimes we must pray alone, seemingly isolated, without words or even the presence of our fellow-men. God speaks to man not only in words but also in silence.

It is not possible to determine the precise effect of prayer in silence. It need lead to no resolutions, no social action; no theological learning nor inspirational thought. Sometimes it merely allows us to become ourselves before the God who gave us our lives, the God to whom our lives are tending.

One does not always come away from time spent with a friend with a plan or a conclusion. One may know only that it was good to have been with each other. Something new about life was learned, not a new concept perhaps but a reminder that friendship is valuable, life joyful, people a comfort. Sometimes one learns nothing more than the fact that one is understood, more than he imagined, better than he hoped.

I learn in friendship that there is another with whom I can laugh and talk, someone to call my name, who knows me, to whom I need not explain myself or defend myself. There is someone I need not fear, a fellow human being who has caught the magic of my life more completely than I could grasp it myself, a friend in whose presence I can be so much myself that I do not feel foolish when I am foolish or petty in my concerns about the small problems of life. All this happens in that personal experience by which one calls another friend, brother, sister.

The contemplative silence of prayer is like this. Sometimes there is nothing to say; one chooses simply *to be* before God. One senses his poverty, his incompleteness, his inarticulateness. He is in need and there is God. A time comes when one is silent because he realizes with painful clarity the fact that he is finite and that his many clever words do not add up to wisdom. A time comes when one knows that his unrelenting efforts have not made for grace and that the labor of a life-time does not measure up to the gift of life he was given without having done a thing to merit it.

There are times when our silence pleads for forgiveness or acceptance; times when our wordlessness is gratitude or adoration. All of a sudden, one becomes aware that he actually *believes* in God with all his heart and that God neither utimately disappoints nor decisively deserts man. Sometimes silence makes us appreciate the daring with which we say "Father" to God and consider ourselves his children. "Father" sometimes becomes the only word silence allows as we express inexpressibly all we feel and want and reach for.

One is silent not only because the rhythm of life requires silence but because the grace of life compels it. Contemplative silence purifies life of its self-deceptions and elevates the human person to the loftiness of God where foolish illusions are dispelled and ego-centric preoccupations exorcized.

A man of faith is silent in a dialogue which engages not only his inner self but the other Self within him. In silence, I accept the fact that I am forceful with Another's strength and that all my loves are linked with Someone who loved me into life though I have never met him. Someone loves my every moment of life and I have never seen him.

Contemplative silence teaches me to affirm myself and yet be humble: for, that which has been given me is more significant than what I can do in return. Silence teaches me to love myself and yet be anxious for my brethren, to live with my talents and to know they are not sufficient.

There is a time for keeping silent. The man who keeps silence as we have described silence is conscious of the urgency of prayer. Life means more to him than its words and deeds. He does not converse only with his fellow-men. There comes a time when his silence speaks and when God who speaks but one Word on man's behalf speaks this Word into the silence of a human heart.

Reflection and silence, prayer and contemplation are the wordless ways by which faith in Life is intensified. In order to believe someone, we must perceive his worth. If life's worth is dissipated, then one has diminished his capacity to consider life worthy of faith or worthy of God. The man who has seen the glory of life disposes himself to behold the glory of God. When he dies, his lips will not speak and his heart will be silent; yet, for the first time, he will know what it means to say everything without saying anything.

Conscience

In their first post-conciliar pastoral letter, *The Church in Our Day*, the American bishops spoke of the inviolability of the human conscience and yet maintained that conscience could not be the ultimate and exclusive norm in man's restless search for truth and innocence. A person who is untrue to his conscience is untrue to himself. But a person who is faithful to unenlightened conscience is faithful to what is less in himself. "Conscience is not only a gift,

inspiring us to virtue and restraining us from vice; it is also a demand that must be accomplished, enlightened, formed, elevated". *(The Church in Our Day)*

We said in our last chapter that there is no freedom without authority. The converse is also true. Nor is there love without obligation or gift without responsibility. Conscience has been given not as an end in itself but as a freedom which seeks a higher freedom, as a means by which love may achieve its most personal expression, if love's obligations are recognized, as a gift which leads to life if it is accepted responsibly.

We live in an age when men wish to rely more fully on their consciences for their judgments about what faith must be for them and how virtue is to be exercised in their lives. This is an encouraging and welcome development. God does exist at the inner core of the person who, if he hears himself correctly, hears God. This issue, however, cannot be settled easily.

Conscience sensitizes a man not only to his personal integrity and identity but also to the indefinable Reality in him over which he has not complete control. Thus, he may feel guilty about something which his culture and his own reasoning process have justified. He can feel compromised in something he considers a benefit to himself. He may sense regret doing those things he was assured were fulfilling; he knows embarrassment even when no one has seen him and when, logically, he ought not be embarrassed. Something in a man makes him disappointed with himself even when no one else is disappointed with him.

In their second post-conciliar pastoral letter, *Human Life in Our Day*, the text of which is an appendix to this book, the American bishops remind us that "God does not leave man to himself but has entered history through a Word which is 'the true light that enlightens all men'; that Word speaks to us and still enlightens us. . ."

Christ is the central point toward which Christian conscience converges. Nothing is more inner to a person than his conscience, nothing so intimately allied with his personal freedom or ultimate identity. And yet Christians believe another Man, whom we confess as Son of God, touched the inner core of each of us with his grace and his mysterious presence, with his penetrating words and his healing death, with his Easter glory and his Spirit of Love. Something happened to human conscience when Christ happened to the human family. The life and destiny of another Man was bound to the life and destiny of conscience.

Conscience was now both a personal prerogative and a Christian reality, a means to self-identity and a way to God, an arbiter in the concrete choice of good or evil and a force tending to absolute Goodness. Something of the mystery of conscience was joined with a community of men, like myself, whose consciences were inviolable and yet who believed that God set the conscience of man free and revealed himself in this further freedom.

There was a conscience of mankind and the Man who made us most aware of this may also have been the Man who made us most aware of God. My conscience cannot, it is true, be directed completely from without, not even by the teaching of the Church of Jesus Christ because this community is not able to teach each man how he must be himself, where the grace of God will meet him, which weaknesses he will suffer, how he must believe in his uniqueness, and what he must do in every case. But something of my conscience is bound up with this community because as a Christian I believe that the wisdom and power of God are revealed more forcefully and clearly in this community than anywhere else. A Christian belongs to the community of the Church because he believes that the mystery of life and the grandeur of love, the meaning of Jesus and the dignity of conscience have been attained by this community in a wholly unique and remarkably catholic manner. This is not triumphalism but the very substance of Christian faith. A Christian cannot expect this community to do everything for him but he is brave enough to assert that alienation from this community is the same as living less. When one has lived more, he cannot bear to live less.

A man who is silent before God need not fear he will easily equate conscience with whim. A man who takes his place in the community of Christ knows that he lives in a fellowship of disciples, many of whom have learned wisdom in silence and prayer. Such a community sheds light, not only on the meaning of Christ's life or the destiny of man but even on the formation of human conscience. A believer surrenders his conscience to no man and yet he knows his conscience requires assistance. The conscience of man is open fully only to God but God, for a Christian, is the One who declared himself in Christ and made a gift of his Spirit to the Church.

The conscience of every Christian is at stake in the life of the Church; the love of the Church is an imperative for the conscience of every Christian. When the true Church speaks, a Christian speaks differently. He does not merely repeat the Church but he has heard the Church in the depths of his heart and the inner recesses of his conscience. And now his definition of faith or his description of love or his awareness of life is not contained fully in his own words nor in the words of the Church but in that silent dialogue of contemplative love which happened within him when the Church of Christ spoke to him and awaited his response.

9
THERE IS A TIME FOR THROWING STONES AWAY

There is a great deal of difference between loss, change, and transformation. A loss is a step back; a change is an opportunity; transformation is a step forward. The common denominator in these three realities is the fact that one must give up something. It is possible for both loss and change to lead to transformation but it is not possible for transformation to occur unless something is lost and something is changed.

All men fear loss and they know they fear it. And yet life, it seems, is a continual process of losing. We lose our youth and our friends, our health and our dreams, our loved ones and eventually our lives. There is no way to hold on to all the values we encounter on the way. Like a child whose arms are filled with gifts, we must let some of them fall out of our keeping as we reach for others. We lose so much in life that some of our fellow-men claim life is only loss, a progressive and inevitable journey into nothingness and amnesia, into absurdity and total darkness. Losing is difficult because in every loss something of myself seems to be gone forever. A man is something when he is young that he cannot be when he grows old. It is possible to become something with a former friend which one cannot become in his absence.

My identity can be so bound up with someone I loved that the separation of death leaves me at a loss as to how I might define myself again. All along the way, I die in a thousand different ways until one day it is not something of mine or someone I loved who dies but it is I who die. Life is indeed a process of losing. Man can hold on to nothing forever, not even himself; he can have no one always, even someone he cannot do without.

All men fear change but few realize it. We are eager for change, especially today, but few people are aware of how unsettling change is. It is no easy thing to change from an infant into a child, to learn to take a step, to remain alone for the first time, to live through the opening day of school.

It is difficult to change into adolescence, to apply for a job, ask for a date, experience failure, become awkward, or learn that reality is not as

pliable as it once seemed to be. It is troublesome to accept middle-age, to see one's options limited and his responsibilities increasing, to know time is running out, to encounter the problem of aging and the attrition of fidelity, to realize at a certain moment that one has done all he is likely to accomplish with his life. It is frightening to find oneself, all of a sudden, old, to be able no longer to do what one was able to do before, to find oneself in the way or out of place, bereft of friends and deprived of those who had a need for the talent and presence of someone the world now deems too old to be of any further assistance.

There is a fear of change because every change involves a re-definition of self and this challenges our deepest resources. Change, however, is not a step back but an opportunity. A child is proud of his ability to walk once he masters is; an adolescent is bewildered at times but he does not wish to be younger than he is; an adult discovers security and happiness, accomplishment and maturity which make him look back on his teen-age years with a wry smile; advancing age provides mellowness and perspective, wisdom and grace, spiritual insight and contentment.

In the process of change, one must do what he did in the process of losing. One must surrender something. But now one lets go of something not because he has no alternative but for the sake of latching onto something else. Change is a chance to grow. But growing is always painful. It means that one must risk loss for the change. "What if I am not loved when I try to love?", an adolescent may wonder. As a child, love was assured; as an adolescent, it must be won. But a child, for whom love is assured, gives little when he loves. An adolescent wishes to give everything, to offer his very self so that love will be not only a gift but a consecration. But an adolescent must risk the loss of himself as he tries to love in this new way. His love may be misinterpreted, mistaken, or even misplaced. There may be no one to love him in return, no one to tell him how much his love meant.

One risks loss for the sake of change when he becomes an adult. A man is nervous on the day of his wedding because he fears he may not be a good husband or a faithful father. If he fails, who is there to help him? A seminarian is anxious on the day of his ordination because he knows the priesthood is beyond him and that failure in his ministry will harm large numbers of people. He will become a scandal for those very people he was ordained to serve. It is easier to be a cadet than a commander-in-the-field, a medical student than a surgeon, an employee than an employer. In all these cases, the stakes are higher, the rewards are greater but the loss is more total. One puts himself on the line and he hopes.

Change is the beginning of transformation if its challenge is met. In order to meet its challenge, however, one must know that there comes a time when one must let go, give up, take a chance, risk failure, surrender comfort, and hope for the best.

Loss occurs almost automatically in life. Youth is taken away whether one wishes this or not, whether one is ready or not. Change is less automatic but life forces change. One may not become an adult but he does stop being an adolescent. If he does not change, he is considered immature. The success of his adolescence is deemed a failure in his adulthood if he relies too much on this former success or previous life style to solve his adult problems and obligations.

There is nothing automatic about transformation. One is not transformed because he reaches a certain age but because he lives by values which renew and refresh the human spirit. One is transformed when he professes faith instead of indecision; when he affirms a hope which cedes neither to naivete nor despair; when he brings love into situations where it was not expected. A man who believes in life is transformed by it; to believe in life one needs faith in it, hope for it, love of it. To believe in life requires all the resources of the human heart; as those resources are expended the exhausted human heart is transformed and perceives more life for further faith, brighter hope, greater love until God himself is touched and the transformation is complete.

There is a time, then, for throwing stones away. A time comes to let go of the pre-conciliar Church for the post-conciliar Church. A time comes when we must hear not only the familiar doctrines but the doctrines which bring us into new life, unfamiliar because it is new but life because it is from the Spirit. A time comes from throwing stones, for letting the water go so that it might be made into wine, for giving away the five barley loaves so that a multitude may be fed, for leaving the security of Nazareth to begin the long journey to Jerusalem.

The life of Jesus was a life of loss, of change, of transformation. Jesus lost his youth and his friends, his disciples and his countrymen. He changed and re-defined himself. He became a child who took a step, an adolescent who was tested by questions and of whom answers were expected rather than given, a young man who saw hatred in the eyes of those he loved and doubt in those he had with him from the beginning.

Jesus changed but transformation eventually required the sacrifice of his life. Jesus did not die because he reached a certain age but because he lived by values so lofty that the life he had was not able to contain them. Jesus was asked to express faith for himself and all human history in an hour when the skies grew dark and God, it seemed, had forsaken him. To Jesus it was given to have hope for the sake of the world's salvation and to love so unreservedly that his love might be an example of God's love for the human family. To remain faithful to this mission demanded all the resources of his mighty heart and his apparently limitless spirit. When Jesus was exhausted in his humanity, the Father touched him with Easter life. And Jesus, who had seemingly lost everything was transformed into the Christ from whom all good things come.

10
THERE IS A TIME FOR HEALING

It is no easy thing to be a human being. A human life is the most unforeseeable and dramatic venture imaginable. Physical laws are stable and animal behavior is predictable. Physical laws do not change and animal life cannot be transformed. The risk of living increases in direct proportion to the quality of life. A physical law remains stationary; even an unusual interruption of it does not affect its intrinsic character. An animal can never be less than animal; it is destined to grow and die with the perfection of its senses, rather than the definition of its identity, at issue in its living.

A human life is radically different. No one knows what a child will become or whether he will even be recognizable in his future. Transformation is at issue in human living. A man can be less than a man or more than a man. He can lose his identity or he can have the inner core of his being renewed. He begins with freedom and is reached by grace, open to love and receptive of faith. He can laugh or weep, hope or worship. In all of this, there is risk, a measure of failure, and yet the possibility of becoming someone who transcends himself and all his limitations. A man may fail and yet succeed in his failure; miss love and yet continue to love; be confined and yet grow in freedom; have all his opportunities denied him and yet believe hopefully in the future. A human life is subject to no control unless it chooses to be controlled; it is capable, as animal life is not, of deciding who its enemies will be or whether it will have any enemies; it has the ability, as animal life does not, of deciding its destiny and of choosing whether it will utilize reason and freedom in the development of its own potential.

Because so much is at stake in the drama of a human life, there is no creature who needs to be healed more often or more deeply than does man.

An animal cannot reach the core of another animal to heal him. But a man can do this for a fellow-man. The things which heal man in his humanity are spiritual realities. A man's humanness is not restored when his senses are repaired or his organic structure restored. An animal can

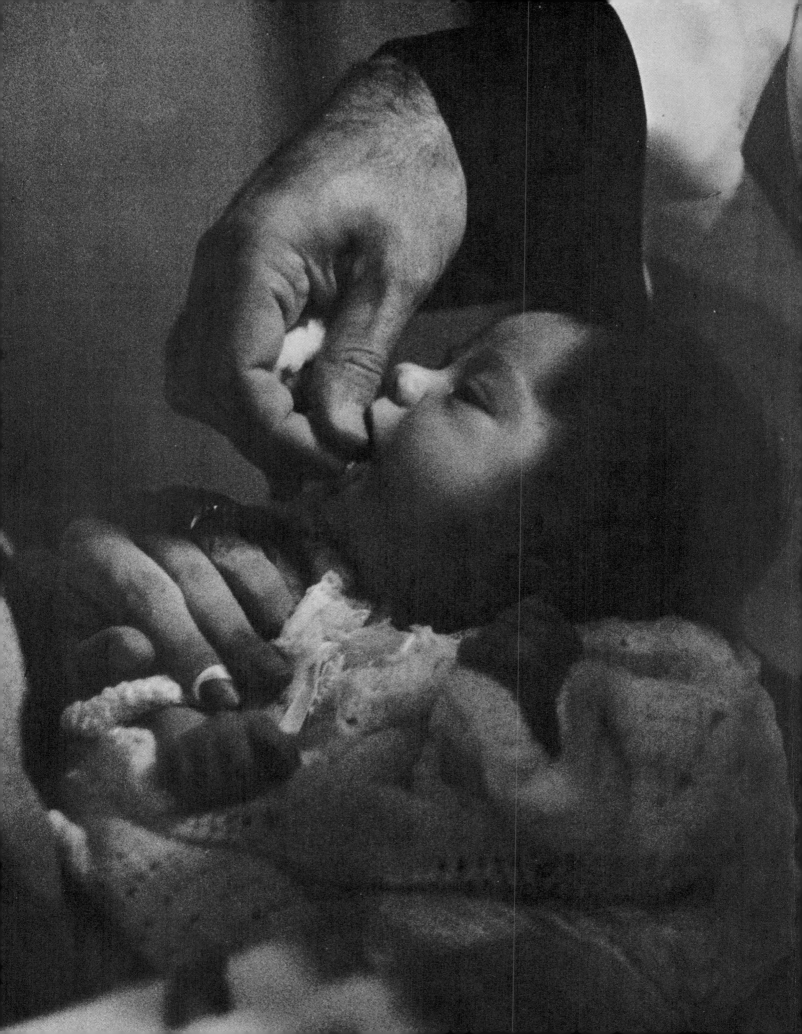

recover its animality by such assistance but with man things are different. The spiritual realities which renew a man are those realities bound up with the life he has which supersedes his physical existence. Only man can be healed by the word another man speaks to him or by the thought another man gives him to think or by the presence of another human being by his side in time of trouble. A word , a thought, or mere presence cannot heal an animal. But they can heal a man.

Only life can heal life; only people can save people. A surgeon may save a man's physical existence but he cannot redeem his humanity. For this, more than surgical instruments are needed; for this, another human life is needed, another human love is required; for this, the words and thoughts and presence of another person are required.

The Church will be the true Church of Jesus, it will justify its existence and become an effective sign of God if it speaks words which heal, if it inspires thoughts which give life, if its presence does more for the world than the world can do for itself.

Modern man yearns for redemption more than revelation; he wants healing more than certitude; salvation more than truth. It is, of course, obvious that redemption is linked with revelation, healing with certitude, salvation with truth. Although both are needed, the emphasis can sometimes shift. A century ago, man's problem with faith was an intellectual problem; men wondered about the relationship of reason with revelation, the compatibility of science and theology, proofs for the existence of God and the marks of the Church. Today it is man's heart and spirit which stumble over faith. A century ago, the faith crisis had much to do with ethics and morality, with behavior and commandments. Today, the faith crisis has more to do with whether there is a worth to the human person and how that worth can be made manifest. Today, personal survival is more critical than personal conduct. Moral misbehavior is not as frightening to us as the thought that there is no point to morality because there is no point to life. We seek a faith to set us free and give us hope rather than for ethical rectitude. We are eager for the belief which makes doctrine believable rather than for the doctrine which does indeed convince a man's intellect but only on condition that his heart has also discovered faith. We search for a faith in life rather than for life's orderly procedure, for a reason to hope rather than for legitimate moral norms. The crisis of faith is a crisis in the human heart which now fears there is no human future for man.

We must avoid unwarranted simplifications. A faith which has no doctrine is sooner or later a vague feeling rather than a saving reality. One must state unequivocally whether or not Jesus is God's Son, whether or not the Eucharist is sacrificial. A faith which has no moral norms is a faith which reaches man in his search for truth but abandons him in his eagerness for innocence. Such a faith is an unfinished faith, an incomplete faith, a disjointed faith.

Granting all this, we make a mistake today when we begin with doctrine and with moral norms or prohibitions rather than with the anxiety in the heart of man which reveals an eagerness for faith but fears there is no faith to sustain its aspirations. When the heart of a believer has reached the heart of his brother, then healing happens and faith is believable. "Heart speaks to heart", as Cardinal Newman expressed it.

Unless this occurs, we offer doctrinal words and wise counsel to another. We convince his mind and direct his actions but we have not given him faith or hope. The search for the faith beneath doctrine and the values beneath norms is the way the search for God is conducted today.

In our effort to make men believe in life so that they will believe in the Lord of life we must consider what life needs rather than what life ought to be. Life needs confidence and hope, preservation and faith. Today is a time for healing.

There are two institutions more capable of an effective mission of healing than any others in our society. The first of these is the family and the second is the Church.

The family heals because it is in the family that life occurs and in the family that love is first offered. When a man finds a family to which he belongs, he finds a home which is his The restoration of the human heart must begin with the family as the unit which reaches man more deeply than any other social unit in which he finds himself. This is why the Church must address itself to the family as the first object of its evangelical mission.

It is because the family is so closely united to life and love that its character is sacred. This is why the Church speaks to man about that act of love from which life comes and about that life in the womb which love must foster and preserve. This is why the Church cannot be indifferent to the way people marry or the reasons why they separate. The mission of the Church is a ministry for men; and men are most fully themselves, most responsive to life, and most faithful to love in the context of the family. There is no man who does not have a family to which he belongs or once belonged, no person who would not rather be reached through his family if this is at all possible. The family is the place where men most often hear the words, think the thoughts, and sense the presence of love.

Life heals life. If the Church can repair man's broken heart or enlighten his confused spirit, it must be because it has life to offer. Unless the Church has life to offer which is different from the life the world gives or even the life the family makes possible, it has no distinctive healing ministry to perform.

The liturgy of the Church is the Church's offer of what it believes to be new life. The sacramental action of the Church is the signification and mediation of this further life. The life the Church seeks through her sacramental liturgy to bestow in its fullness is the life of Jesus, the Christ.

Because her sacraments are life-oriented, the Church begins with baptism which is called a new birth and completes them with the Eucharist which is a celebration of the life, death, and Easter presence of Jesus. Because her sacraments are life-seeking, she first uses water, from which physical life traced its origins, and fulfills

them with the mystery of that sacred body and blood on which life depends.

But life must not only begin or achieve its accomplishment; it stands in need of restoration and healing. The Church celebrates supplementary sacraments as her way of saying that we have been forgiven our trespasses and that the sickness which seems to signal the end of all healing is open to the further healing and fuller life of God. She tells us in her sacrament of marriage that marital life and love are linked with Christ, and in her sacrament of ordination that the community life and love of the Church will endure.

The Church seeks to heal not only in her liturgy but in her teaching. She composed and kept in existence the Scripture whose words have healed more men than anything else written in human history. This Scripture is given its privileged moment in the liturgy. The Church seeks in the power of the Spirit and assisted by the prayer of her members to enlighten the human conscience with healing wisdom. The conscience of man is able to do less than it is able to do unless it can be inspired with nobler life and more comprehensive love. The Church's doctrine speaks of grace as healing grace and of God as the One who sent his Son to reconcile us to one another and to the Father in the healing power of his forgiving love and divine life. The Church maintains that the healing of the human heart depends on belief in the God of life, hope in the endless future of man, and love which goes beyond the loves of each human life to the inexhaustible Love at the heart of reality.

The point of the Church's liturgy and sacraments, of her doctrine and life is healing. Her worship is composed of healing words; her creeds, of healing thoughts; her communal life, of a healing Presence. And man is healed in his humanity, as we said before, by words, thoughts, and presence. The crisis in the life of the Church today is a crisis about whether or not the communal structure of the Church's life and love threatens more than it heals or, if it heals, whether it can heal more effectively than it does. The purpose of reform and renewal is the discovery of the deeper dimensions of the Church's healing power.

But why has the Church undertaken such a mission? Why does it think it has a life to offer and a love to speak of which are not available to the human family without the Church? It thinks this because it believes the life of Jesus is bound up with its life in an altogether unique manner; it believes that Jesus will be less alive in the world unless a community of his disciples, inspired by the Spirit and commissioned by Christ himself, declares the existence of a way of living which the human family is not aware of on its own. The Gospel is revelation rather than discovery. It tells man about something he would not have come upon had he not explicitly encountered it. This Gospel forms a community and requires a community for its own life. Jesus healed men and redeemed the Church; the Church seeks to speak of this healing and redemption which transform the heart of man in a way nothing else can.

There is a time for healing in the life of man. The Church intends to be there when men feel they have sustained a sickness unto death. There was a time when the wounds from the cross were healed and when the heart of Jesus was made whole again. There is a time to be healed even from death, as Easter assures us.

The Church knows that the heart of man is not alive in doubt, active in despair, vital in hatred. It offers life again by giving reasons for faith and hope, for love and healing when men have run out of reasons and are on the verge of thinking their future is less than it really is.

There was a time, the Church confesses, when God's own Word healed us; a time when God's thinking was committed to our keeping as the Son revealed to us the God he knew as Father; a time when the presence of God was made a moment in our history in the flesh and blood of the Jesus men crucified and God healed.

There was a time when the human heart was healed by the spiritual realities of the words and thought and presence of life's Creator and the heart's Savior. And there will come a time when God shall come again, summing up our history and healing us with Life no death can threaten and Love no man can refuse.

11
THERE IS A TIME FOR WAR

For the first time in human history, men are able to ask realistically whether there need ever again be a time for war. During this century, men developed international institutions whose purpose was the salvation of succeeding generations from the scourge of war. The present young generation has made us acutely aware that wars can be prevented and that the conscience of mankind demands that they be eliminated. Pope Paul VI, in his speech to the United Nations, reminded its delegates:

. . . You deal here above all with human life and human life is sacred; no one may dare offend against it.

Because of this, he pleaded in the name of "the dead who fell in the terrible wars of the past", in the name of "the youth of the present generation who legitimately expect a better human race", in the name of "the poor, the disinherited, the suffering, of those who long for justice . . . never one against the other, never again, never more . . . no more war, never again war".

Paul warned the United Nations that "the hour has struck for our conversion, for personal transformation, for internal renewal". It is this dimension of the problem of war which we must not overlook. War is the result of our divided hearts, our unhealed spirits, our despairs and our doubts, our hostilities and our hatreds. War is not a disease but a symptom of the sickness in the heart of man. It is the end product of every choice we make of objects over persons, of exploitation over love, of prestige over life.

We must not assume that we are blameless while other men wage war or that we are, in every case, the innocent victims of war. We are often those who have added to the burden of the world's evil and inflamed the rage by which Cain continues to slaughter Abel. When it comes to an assessment of why there are wars, there is no man without sin in our midst.

We bear a collective responsibility before the tribunal of God for war's existence. There has always been a time for war because we have loved darkness more than light, pointed out the splinter in our brother's eye neglecting the beam in our own, and filled our days with envy and

pride, with selfishness and fear. In the stark face of war, man often beholds the bleakness of his own heart and the vision is so terrible that he seeks to blame everyone but himself. Wars do not happen; they are made.

Until men believe in life, there shall be wars, evermore savage, evermore deadly. Until men find a faith which leads them to consecrate their lives to peace or a hope which brings them to rely on the moral force of human life or a love which transforms, there shall be wars and even perhaps one day a war which destroys the planet.

There is a time for war because each man finds in his life a time for hatred. We bear arms against one another because we harbored first the desire to injure one another in subtler ways. Before we use a weapon, we have many times wished that a neighbor might fail, rejoiced as an enemy suffered, or longed that a friend might be less than we are.

War is the external sign of that evil in man's heart which he is often unwilling to admit. As each of us searches for someone to blame for war, God might well remind us "That man is You".

It is unlikely that a day will dawn soon when sin is no more. So long as this is true, we all live under the threat of war. It may happen, however, that international institutions and the conscience of mankind will end all military hostilities. We must not despair of this possibility. When we accomplish this, however, we shall have healed only a symptom, as we have said. But the healing of a symptom does bring a measure of relief. The healing of a symptom can lead us to become more conscious of the disease which caused it.

Of all the ideals men in our day cherish, peace in the world is first in their order of priorities. Christ is acknowledged by us Christians as the Prince of Peace. The beatitudes he preached remind us of our individual complicity in collective guilt. Each one of us is encouraged to be "poor in spirit", to "hunger and thirst for righteousness", to be "merciful", "pure in heart", "peacemakers". The final judgment of history, we are told, will concern itself with our acceptance or refusal of brotherly love. "I was hungry and you did not give me to eat . . . I was a stranger and you did not take me home . . . that which you did to one of these least brethren of mine, you did to me."

Christians, therefore, are charged to attack the root cause of war; they are commissioned to keep alive for men the message of peace their Master preached. We are not worthy of the name Christian unless we seek to renew our hearts and reform the world simultaneously.

Paul VI called development the new name for peace. War will plague man so long as social justice is denied him. The Gospel refuses to define our neighbor in racial or ethnic terms. Our neighbor is the one nearby or the one far away, the one who needs nothing and the one who needs everything. Our neighbor is everyone or anyone. Who then is not our neighbor? By what standard do we decide to deny justice to one man and to render it to another? Human life is human life. It is sacred for every man, expendable for no man.

There is a time for war because men have been conscious of their needs but not of their brother's needs. There is a time for war because men formulate definitions of brotherhood which exclude those who remain our brothers nonetheless. There is a time for war because men believe in their own lives and not in human life, in their right to be loved but not in their responsibility to love in return.

12
THERE IS A TIME FOR PEACE

Life reveals its mystery to us in simple realities. Life is a child's smile and a distant star, a flower that all of a sudden attracts our attention, and the sound of our name on the lips of those we love.

Life is a time for tears and for losing, for quiet suffering and anguished pain. But life, as we know, gives birth to more life, leads to love, causes us to laugh, fills us with creative silence, transforms us if we do not despair, and heals us even when we thought we might not recover. Life sometimes finds time for war but it offers peace more often.

Life may be so bitter that we can regret having been given it as a gift. It is sometimes so tragic that we have no wish to continue. This tragedy comes not only from our dramatic problems but from the accumulation of our daily disappointments. Far more frequently, life is capable of making us grateful for being alive. It renders us serene in the hour before dawn and in the splendor of sunrise. It makes us nostalgic every autumn with the wordless beauty of its dying glory. Life takes us every day into the tranquility of sunset and the magic of night. Life assures us of its worth every time we see a sleeping infant; it convinces us somehow that things will work out correctly. Life makes men consider God, his creative Love, the Spirit of Peace, the crucified Christ.

There is a time for peace and it is always a simple time. It numbers its moments in those fleeting experiences we live, never hold on to but never forget. It is measured in those many moments when we are certain something wonderful will happen to us after we die, moments when no one seems unworthy of love, and when everything we touch convinces us that God must exist and surely he loves us. If he did not, why would we think of him as love, and turn to love him when there is still love in our hearts after all our created loves have been spoken? God is someone to thank for everything always.

A time for peace comes to every man who learns to make like uncomplicated. It is given to a Christian when he remembers God became a child and that God's only Son felt human brotherhood with us.

A time for peace is God's gift to those who see life as a vast, unexplored light, bounded by no horizons, open to its Creator. It is Christ's grace for those who can speak their hope in turmoil:

In spite of it all, I lived. I took my chances and made risky decisions. I always found someone to love, someone who gave me hope. My faith in God tells me I will never run out of people to love, never meet a disaster so total that I will be justified in my despair. I have lived and I cannot accept the fact that there was no point to this. I have lived and I refuse to believe that there is not a God to hear the story of my life when that life is finished. I refuse to believe that no one kept time for the world and that there is not someone to keep my heart when I have nowhere else to place it. My courage came from life, my faith from a refusal to die, my hope from the moments of peace and love I found. All the things I never expected, happened. I did not expect to be alive or expect that there had to be God. I did not expect love and I did not expect a human family beyond the family I knew as a child. For these reasons, I believe there will always be a time for peace and that one day peace will never end.

A Christian has no faith in war, no faith in death, no faith in doubt, no faith in despair, no faith in hatred; for God is the only One in whom his faith is fully spoken. And God is a God of peace and of life, inviting faith, giving hope, loving without limit.

When Christians have faith in peace, they have faith in that day when men will never again bear arms against one another. They have faith that the men who crucified Christ will one day repent and that Christ shall forgive them. They have faith that man's journey toward freedom and love will continue in spite of all the setbacks, all the disasters, all the mishaps, all the blunders.

Christians keep faith with men who choose not to fight in a war because it violates their conscience; they have faith that one day men will depersonalize war and wage war against poverty and disease, ignorance and evil rather than against their brothers and sisters. Christians believe their Church will speak the message it must speak and that most men will somehow hear it.

There is a time for peace because birth continues to happen and because more people treasure life than despise it.

There is a time for peace because people find time to speak their values to one another, to love one another, to laugh with one another, and to tell one another that they have wept.

There is a time for peace because men build better than they destroy and because they wish to pray even when they do not.

There is a time for peace because people believe in conscience and hope for a better future.

There is a time for peace because men are happier when they heal one another than when they injure one another.

There is a time for peace because no one really wants war and because the Church has survived and the Gospel has not been forgotten.

There is a time for peace because men know they are brothers and because they keep looking for reasons to have faith in God even while they deny him.

There is a time for peace even after we die, even after we sustain all the pain and waste of death. For, life was given to be accomplished and we all die with promises to keep.

There is a time for peace because once in human history there was time for the human heart.

"HUMAN LIFE IN OUR DAY"
Pastoral Letter of The American Bishops

INTRODUCTORY STATEMENT

We honor God when we reverence human life. When human life is served, man is enriched and God is acknowledged. When human life is threatened, man is diminished and God is less manifest in our midst.

A Christian defense of life should seek to clarify in some way the relationship between the love of life and the worship of God. One cannot love life unless he worships God, at least implicitly, nor worship God unless he loves life.

The purpose of this pastoral letter of the United States bishops is precisely the doctrine and defense of life. Our present letter follows the moral principles set forth in the *Pastoral Constitution on the Church in the Modern World* issued by Vatican Council II. It presupposes the general doctrine of the Church which we explored in our pastoral letter *The Church in Our Day*. It responds to the encyclical *Humanae Vitae* in this same context.

We are prompted to speak this year in defense of life for reasons of our pastoral obligation to dialogue within the believing community concerning what faith has to say in response to the threat to life in certain problems of the family and of war and peace.

We also choose to speak of life because of the needed dialogue among all men of faith. This is particularly necessary among Christians and all believers in God, and between believers and all who love life if peace is to be secured and life is to be served. There is evidence that many men find difficulty in reconciling their love for life with worship of the Lord of life.

On the other hand, it is becoming clear that the believer and the humanist have common concerns for both life and peace. For example, an agnostic philosopher, much listened to by contemporary students, has this to say:

"Why do not those who represent the traditions of religion and humanism speak up and say that there is no deadlier sin than love for death and contempt for life? Why not encourage our best brains—scientists, artists, educators—to make suggestions on how to arouse and stimulate love for life as opposed to love for gadgets? . . . Maybe it is too late. Maybe the neutron bomb which leaves entire cities intact, but without life, is to be the symbol of our civilization" (Erich Fromm: *The Heart of Man: Its Genius for Good and Evil*).

The defense of life provides a starting point, then, for positive dialogue between Christians and humanists. Christians bring to the dialogue on the defense of life a further motivation. We are convinced that belief in God is intimately bound up with devotion to life. God is the ultimate source of life, His Son its Redeemer, so that denial of God undermines the sanctity of life itself.

Our pastoral letter will emphasize the maturing of life in the family and the development of life in a peaceful world order. Threats to life are most effectively confronted by an appeal to Christian conscience. We pray that our words may join us in common cause with all who reverence life and seek peace. We pray further that our efforts may help join all men in common faith before God Who "gives freely and His gift is eternal life" (Rm. 6,23).

The Christian Family

The attitude man adopts toward life helps determine the

person he becomes. In the family, man and life are first united. In the family, the person becomes the confident servant of life and life becomes the servant of man. The Church must make good her belief in human life and her commitment to its development by active as well as doctrinal defense of the family and by practical witness to the values of family life.

The Church thinks of herself as a family, the family of God and, so, is the more solicitous for the human family. She sees Christian marriage as a sign of the union between Christ and the Church (cf. Eph. 5, 31-32), a manifestation to history of the "genuine nature of the Church" (*Gaudium et Spes,* 48). Christian married love is "caught up into divine love and is governed and enriched by Christ's redeeming power and the saving activity of the Church" (*Gaudium et Spes,* 48). No institution or community in human history has spoken more insistently and profoundly than the Church of the dignity of marriage.

It is in terms of Christ and of salvation history, never of sociology alone, that the Church thinks of marriage. That is the point of her positive teachings on the sanctity, the rights and the duties of the married state; it is also the point of her occasional strictures, as when Vatican Council II realistically cautions that "married love is too often profaned by excessive self-love, the worship of pleasure, and illicit practices against human generation" (*Gaudium et Spes,* 47).

The family fulfills its promise when it reinforces fidelity to life and hope in its future. The values of fidelity and hope, essential to human life and Christian love, are sometimes weakened even while men continue to think all is well. Such is often the case in our times. Fidelity and hope are especially threatened when the family is considered largely in terms of the pleasures or conveniences it provides for the individual or in terms of its economic or political potential. Christians should be the first to promote material improvement and provide for the family structure, but they must never measure the worth of the family nor the purpose of family life by these standards alone.

For the believer, the family is the place where God's image is reproduced in His creation. The family is the community within which the person is realized, the place where all our hopes for the future of the person are nourished. The family is a learning experience in which fidelity is fostered, hope imparted and life honored; it thus increases the moral resources of our culture and, more importantly, of the person. The family is a sign to all mankind of fidelity to life and of hope in the future which become possible when persons are in communion with one another; it is a sign to believers of the depth of this fidelity and this hope when these center on God; it is a sign to Christians of the fidelity and hope which Christ communicates as the elder brother of the family of the Church for which He died (cf. Eph. 5,25).

The Family: A Force for Life

It is an unfortunate fact that in all times some men have acted against life. The forms of the threat have varied; some of these endure to this day. Since the family is the source of life, no act against life is more hostile than one which occurs within the family. By such an act, life is cancelled out within that very community whose essential purposes include the gift of life to the world and the service of life in fidelity and hope.

For all these reasons, the Christian family is called more now than ever to a prophetic mission, a witness to the primacy of life and the importance of whatever preserves life. The Christian family therefore occupies a pre-eminent place in our renewed theology, particularly the theology of marriage and of the vocation of the laity. Christian families are called to confront the world with the full reality of human love and proclaim to the world the mystery of divine love as these are revealed through the family.

The prophetic mission of the family obliges it to fidelity to conjugal love in the face of the compromises and infidelities condoned in our culture. Its prophetic mission obliges the family to valiant hope in life, contradicting whatever forces seek to prevent, destroy or impair life. In its emphasis on the virtues of fidelity and hope, so essential to the prophetic witness of the family, Christian sexual morality derives therefore not from the inviolability of generative biology, but ultimately from the sanctity of life itself and the nobility of human sexuality.

The Christian ascetic of chastity, within and outside marriage, honors the sanctity of life and protects the dignity of human sexuality. Were there no Revelation nor religion, civilization itself would require rational discipline of the sexual instinct. Revelation, however, inspires chastity with more sublime purposes and creative power. In chaste love, the Christian, whether his vocation be to marriage or to celibacy, expresses love for God Himself. In the case of spouses, marital chastity demands not the contradiction of sexuality but its ordered expression in openness to life and fidelity to love, which means also openness and faithfulness to God.

These considerations enter into the definition of responsible parenthood. The decision to give life to another person is the responsibility, under God, of the spouses who, in effect, ask the Creator to commit to their care the formation of a child (cf. *Gaudium et Spes,* 50). The fact that the decision touches upon human life and the human person is an indication of the reverence in which it must be made; the fact that the decision involves openness to God's creative power and providential love demands that it be unselfish, free from all calculation inconsistent with generosity.

Responsible parenthood, as the Church understands it, places on the properly formed conscience of spouses all the judgments, options and choices which add up to the awesome decision to give, postpone or decline life. The final decision may sometimes involve medical, economic, sociological or psychological considerations, but in no case can it deliberately choose objective moral disorder. If it is to be responsible, it cannot be the result of mere caprice nor of superficial judgments concerning relative values as between persons and things, between life and its conveniences.

Marital love, then, in its deepest meaning relates not only to the birth and rearing of children within the family society, but to the growth and well-being of human society on its every level and in its every aspect. It relates at the same time to the eternal life of those who choose marriage as their way to salvation. It is within this perspective of a total vision of man and not merely of isolated family considerations, narrowly conceived, that Pope Paul, drawing extensively on the content of Vatican Council II, has written his encyclical *Humanae Vitae.*

The Encyclical and Its Content

The *Pastoral Constitution on the Church in the Modern World* provides the theological framework within which Pope Paul works out the teaching set forth in *Humanae Vitae:*

"Therefore when there is question of harmonizing conjugal love with the responsible transmission of life, the moral aspect of any procedure does not depend solely on sincere intentions or on an evaluation of motives. It must be determined by objective standards. These, based on the nature of the human person and his acts, preserve the full sense of mutual self-giving and human procreation in the context of true love. Such a goal cannot be achieved unless the virtue of conjugal chastity is sincerely practiced. Relying on these principles, sons of the Church may not undertake methods of regulating procreation which are found blameworthy by the teaching authority of the Church in its unfolding of the divine law.

"Everyone should be persuaded that human life and the task of transmitting it are not realities bound up with this world alone. Hence they cannot be measured or perceived only in terms of it, but always have a bearing on the eternal destiny of men" (*Gaudium et Spes,* 51).

Pope Paul speaks of conjugal love as "fully human," "a very special form of personal friendship," "faithful and exclusive until death," "a source of profound and lasting happiness." Such love, however, "is not exhausted by the communion between husband and wife, but is destined to continue, raising up new lives." There is an "objective moral order established by God" which requires that "each and every marriage act must remain open to the transmission of life."

Both conciliar and papal teaching, therefore, emphasize that the interrelation between the unitive meaning and the procreative meaning of marriage is impaired, even contradicted, when acts expressive of marital union are performed without love on the one hand and without openness to life on the other. Consistent with this, the encyclical sees the use of the periodic rhythms of nature, even though such use avoids rather than prevents conception, as morally imperfect if its motivation is primarily refusal of life rather than the human desire to share love within the spirituality of responsible parenthood.

The encyclical *Humanae Vitae* is not a negative proclamation, seeking only to prohibit artificial methods of contraception. In full awareness of population problems and family anxieties, it is a defense of life and of love, a defense which challenges the prevailing spirit of the times. Long-range judgments may well find the moral insights of the encyclical prophetic and its world-view providential. There is already evidence that some peoples in economically under-developed areas may sense this more than those conditioned by the affluence of a privileged way of life.

The encyclical is a positive statement concerning the nature of conjugal love and responsible parenthood, a statement which derives from a global vision of man, an integral view of marriage, and the first principles, at least, of a sound sexuality. It is an obligatory statement, consistent with moral convictions rooted in the traditions of Eastern and Western Christian faith; it is an authoritative statement solemnly interpreting imperatives which are divine rather than ecclesiastical in origin. It presents without ambiguity, doubt or hesitation the authentic teaching of the Church concerning the objective evil of that contraception which closes the marital act to the transmission of life, deliberately making it unfruitful. United in collegial solidarity with the Successor of Peter, we proclaim this doctrine.

The encyclical reminds us that the use of the natural rhythms never involves a direct positive action against the possibility of life; artificial contraception always involves a direct positive action against the possibility of life. Correspondence with the natural rhythms remains essentially attuned to the unitive and procreative intent of the conjugal act even when the spouses are aware of the silence of nature to life.

There are certain values which may not oblige us always to act on their behalf, but we are prohibited from ever acting directly against them by positive acts. Truth is such a value; life is surely another. It is one thing to say that an action against these values is inculpable, diminished in guilt, or subjectively defensible; it is quite another to defend it as objectively virtuous.

The Church's teaching on the moral means to responsible parenthood presupposes certain positive values. One of these is that Christian marriage involves an ever-maturing mutuality between husband and wife, a constantly increasing awareness of the manner in which the total nuptial relationship parallels and symbolizes the love-sharing and life-giving union between Christ and His Church. The unitive and creative values symbolized by sexual expression permeate marriage in its every aspect. This consideration becomes more important as the years of married life go by, especially when changes in society give couples longer years of leisure together after their children begin to live on their own. This explains the importance that couples be united from the beginning of their love by common interests and shared activities which will intensify their nuptial relationship and insure its unity against disruption because of disappointment in one or another of their hopes.

No one pretends that responsible parenthood or even fidelity to the unitive love of marriage, as these are understood by the Church, is easy of attainment without prayerful discipline. Recourse to natural rhythms, for example, presents problems which the Holy Father has asked medical science to help solve. Chastity, as other virtues, is not mastered all at once or without sacrifice. It may involve failures and success, declines and growth, regressions in the midst of progress. A hierarchy of values that reflects a conformity to the example of Christ is neither easily achieved nor insured against loss. Moreover, Christians, however many their failures, will neither expect nor wish the Church to obscure the moral ideal in the light of which they press forward to perfection.

In the pursuit of the ideal of chastity, again as of every other virtue to which he is bound, the Christian must never lose heart; least of all can he pretend that compromise is conquest. At all times, his mind and heart will echo St. Paul: "Not that I have become perfect yet; I have not yet won, but I am still running, trying to capture the prize for which Christ Jesus captured me" (Phil. 3,12). In no case, does he suppose that the Church, in proposing such goals, teaches erroneously and needlessly burdens her members.

They are quite right who insist that the Church must labor to heal the human condition by more than word and precept alone if she wishes her preaching to be taken seriously. All the moral teaching of the Church proposes objective standards difficult to attain: of honesty, respect for other people's property and lives, social justice, integrity in public office, devotion to learning, to service, to God. These standards demand of those to whom they are preached renunciations, frequently against the grain, but creative in their final effect. They also demand of those who preach these ideals that they, too, play their full part in the struggle against the social evils which obstruct their attainment.

We shall consider later in this letter some of our pastoral responsibilties toward the promotion of distributive justice, the rights and stability of the family, and the consequent social climate favorable to marriage morality. In the meantime, the Church, when she fulfills her prophetic role of preaching moral ideals and social reform, must do so with all the patience that the work of teaching requires (cf. 2 Tim. 4,2).

The existence of the Sacrament of Penance in the Church is an indication that Christian ideals are not easy to achieve nor, once achieved, ours forever. The Church cannot, however, compromise the ideal. She is bound to teach it as it is.

The Encyclical and Conscience

Developing last year the teaching of the Council on the nature of the Church, we spoke of the reciprocal claims of conscience and authority in the Christian community as Christ called it into being. We noted that conscience "though it is inviolable is not a law unto itself"; that "the distinction between natural religion and revealed lies in this: that one has a subjective authority, and the other an objective," though both invoke conscience. We recalled that "God does not leave man to himself but has entered history through a Word which is 'the true light that enlightens all men'; that Word speaks to us and still enlightens us in the Church of Jesus Christ ;which carries the double burden of human conscience and divine authority."

These wider questions of conscience, its nature, witness, aberrations and claims, above all its formation, are presupposed in this encyclical as in any papal or conciliar decisions on moral teaching. We recognize the role of conscience as a "practical dictate," not a teacher of doctrine.

Thomas Aquinas describes conscience as the practical judgment or dictate of reason, by which we judge what here and now is to be done as being good, or to be avoided as evil. Vatican Council II says that a man is not to be forced to act in a manner contrary to his conscience (cf. *Declaration on Religious Freedom,* 3). This is certainly true in any conflict between a practical dictate of conscience and a legislative or administrative decree of any superior.

However, when it is a question of the Pope's teaching, as distinct from a decree or order, on a matter bound up with life and salvation, the question of conscience and its formation takes on quite different perspectives and dimensions. Cardinal Newman puts it in strong terms: ". . . I have to say again, lest I should be misunderstood, that when I speak of conscience, I mean conscience truly so called. When it has the right of opposing the supreme, though not infallible Authority of the Pope, it must be something more than that miserable counterfeit which, as I have said above, now goes by the name. If in a particular case it is to be taken as a sacred and sovereign monitor, its dictate, in order to prevail against the voice of the Pope, must follow upon serious thought, prayer, and all available means of arriving at a right judgment on the matter in question. And further, obedience to the Pope is what is called 'in possession'; that is, the *onus probandi* (burden of proof) of establishing a case against him lies, as in all cases of exception, on the side of conscience. Unless a man is able to say to

himself, as in the Presence of God, that he must not, and dare not, act upon the Papal injunction, he is bound to obey it and would commit a great sin in disobeying it. *Prima facie* it is his bounden duty, even from a sentiment of loyalty, to believe the Pope right and to act accordingly . . ." (*A Letter to the Duke of Norfolk*).

Humanae Vitae does not discuss the question of the good faith of those who make practical decisions in conscience against what the Church considers a divine law and the Will of God. The encyclical does not undertake to judge the consciences of individuals but to set forth the authentic teaching of the Church which Catholics believe interprets the divine law to which conscience should be conformed.

The *Pastoral Constitution on the Church in the Modern World* reminds us that "in their manner of acting, spouses should be aware that they cannot proceed arbitrarily. They must always be governed according to a conscience dutifully conformed to the divine law itself, and should be submissive toward the Church's teaching office, which authentically interprets that law in the light of the Gospel. That divine law reveals and protects the integral meaning of conjugal love and impels it toward a truly human fulfillment" (*Gaudium et Spes,* 50). We must not suppose that there is such conflict between authority and freedom, between objective values and subjective fulfillment, that one can only prevail by the elimination of the other.

Married couples faced with conflicting duties are often caught in agonizing crises of conscience. For example, at times it proves difficult to harmonize the sexual expression of conjugal love with respect for the life-giving power of sexual union and the demands of responsible parenthood. Pope Paul's encyclical and the commentaries of the international episcopates on it are sensitive as are we to these painful situations. Filled with compassion for the human condition the Holy Father offers counsel which we make our own:

"Let married couples, then, face up to the efforts needed, supported by the faith and hope which do not disappoint . . . because God's love has been poured into our hearts through the Holy Spirit. Who has been given to us; let them implore divine assistance by persevering prayer; above all, let them draw from the source of grace and charity in the Eucharist. And if sin should still keep its hold over them, let them not be discouraged, but rather have recourse with humble perseverance to the mercy of God, which is poured forth in the Sacrament of Penance" (*Humanae Vitae,* 25).

We feel bound to remind Catholic married couples, when they are subjected to the pressures which prompt the Holy Father's concern, that however circumstances may reduce moral guilt, no one following the teaching of the Church can deny the objective evil of artificial contraception itself. With pastoral solicitude we urge those who have resorted to artificial contraception never to lose heart but to continue to take full advantage of the strength which comes from the Sacrament of Penance and the grace, healing, and peace in the Eucharist. May we all be mindful of the invitation of Jesus: "The man who comes to me I will never turn away" (Jn. 6,37). Humility, awareness of our pilgrim state, a willingness and determination to grow in the likeness of the Risen Christ will help to restore direction of purpose and spiritual stability.

Negative Reactions to the Encyclical

The position taken by the Holy Father in his encyclical troubled many. The reasons for this are numerous. Not a few had been led and had led others to believe that a contrary decision might be anticipated. The mass media which largely shape public opinion have, as the Holy Father himself pointed out, at times amplified the voices which are contrary to the voice of the Church. Then, too, doctrine on this point has its effect not only on the intellects of those who hear it but on their deepest emotions; it is hardly surprising that negative reactions have ranged from sincere anguish to angry hurt or bitter disappointment, even among devout believers. Finally, a decision on a point so long uncontroverted and only recently confronted by new questions was bound to meet with mixed reactions.

That tensions such as these should arise within the household of the faith is not surprising and need not be scandalous. The Holy Father frankly confessed that his teaching would not be easily received by all. Some reactions were regrettable, however, in the light of the explicit teaching of Vatican Council II concerning the obligation of Catholics to assent to papal teaching even when it is not presented with the seal of infallibility. The Council declared:

"In matters of faith and morals, the bishops speak in the name of Christ and the faithful are to accept their teaching and adhere to it with a religious assent of soul. This religious submission of will and of mind must be shown in a special way to the authentic teaching authority of the Roman Pontiff, even when he is not speaking *ex cathedra*. That is, it must be shown in such a way that his supreme magisterium is acknowledged with reverence, the judgments made by him are sincerely adhered to, according to his manifest mind and will. His mind and will in the matter may be known chiefly either from the character of the documents, from his frequent repetition of the same doctrine, or from his manner of speaking" (*Lumen Gentium*, 25).

Pope Paul has recalled this obligation several times with respect to his encyclical on the regulation of birth, beginning when he exhorted priests "to be the first to give, in the exercise of your ministry, the example of loyal internal and external obedience to the teaching authority of the Church" (*Humanae Vitae*, 28).

Norms of Licit Theological Dissent

There exist in the Church a lawful freedom of inquiry and of thought and also general norms of licit dissent. This is particularly true in the area of legitimate theological speculation and research. When conclusions reached by such professional theological work prompt a scholar to dissent from non-infallible received teaching the norms of licit dissent come into play. They require of him careful respect for the consciences of those who lack his special competence or opportunity for judicious investigation. These norms also require setting forth his dissent with propriety and with regard for the gravity of the matter and the deference due the authority which has pronounced on it.

The reverence due all sacred matters, particularly questions which touch on salvation, will not necessarily require the responsible scholar to relinquish his opinion but certainly to propose it with prudence born of intellectual grace and a Christian confidence that the truth is great and will prevail.

When there is question of theological dissent from non-infallible doctrine, we must recall that there is always a presumption in favor of the magisterium. Even non-infallible authentic doctrine, though it may admit of development or call for clarification or revision, remains binding and carries with it a moral certitude, especially when it is addressed to the universal Church, without ambiguity, in response to urgent questions bound up with faith and crucial to morals. The expression of theological dissent from the magisterium is in order only if the reasons are serious and well-founded, if the manner of the dissent does not question or impugn the teaching authority of the Church and is such as not to give scandal.

Since our age is characterized by popular interest in theological debate, and given the realities of modern mass media, the ways in which theological dissent may be effectively expressed, in a manner consistent with pastoral solicitude, should become the object of fruitful dialogue between bishops and theologians. These have their diverse ministries in the Church, their distinct responsibilities to the faith and their respective charisms.

Even responsible dissent does not excuse one from faithful presentation of the authentic doctrine of the Church when one is performing a pastoral ministry in Her name.

We count on priests, the counsellors of persons and families, to heed the appeal of Pope Paul that they "expound the Church's teaching on marriage without ambiguity"; that they "diminish in no way the saving teaching of Christ," but "teach married couples the indispensable way of prayer . . . without ever allowing them to be discouraged by their weakness" (*Humanae Vitae*, 29). We commend to confessors, as does Pope Paul, the example of the Lord Himself, who was indeed intransigent with evil, but merciful toward individuals.

Family Spirituality

Our concern for family life must extend far beyond the publication of pastoral letters. We pledge ourselves to cooperate in multiplying ways and means toward the renewal of the family and the enhancing of its prestige. Specifically, we shall increase our encouragement in the dioceses and the nation of programs undertaken by apostolic groups whose objective is the natural and spiritual strengthening of the Christian family.

Because of the primacy of the spiritual in all that makes for renewal, we give top priority to whatever may produce a sound "family spirituality." Family prayer, above all that which derives its content and spirit from the liturgy, and other devotions, particularly the Rosary; family reading of the Scriptures; family attendance at Mass and reception of Communion; family retreats, days of recollection and other special devotions; the observance of occasions of spiritual significance for members of the household—all these will increase the awareness of the family that it is the "Church in miniature."

For these reasons, we welcome the work of those theologians who are preparing a modern and valid ascetical theology of marriage. We recall gratefully the spiritual emphasis in many family-life programs, national and local, whose primary focus of concern has been the theology of the Christian family.

To prepare future spouses more adequately we recommend specialized team-efforts in their behalf on the part of pastors of souls and qualified counsellors, including devout married couples. Such projects will give engaged couples the benefit of human wisdom and of Christian spirituality in the planning of their home, the founding of a family, the education of children, and all that makes for fidelity and hope in their lives together.

We endorse the establishment of diocesan family life centers throughout the country so that Christian couples, physicians, psychologists, sociologists and priests may cooperate in implementing responsible parenthood in accordance with the principles enunciated in *Humanae Vitae*. On the national level, in response to the Holy Father's request for scientific research into effective and moral means of family planning, we bishops in the United States intend to establish an independent, non-denominational, non-profit foundation which will sponsor scientific research resulting in conclusions which will be helpful to doctors, educators and, ultimately, spouses in licit family planning.

The responsibility of our Family Life Division to provide information, educational tools and guidance in the face of the mounting problems of family life will make it an increasing source of service to diocesan family programs. We also hope to see established centers of education in family life under the auspices of local medical schools or doctors' guilds together with collegiate or adult education progams, and the chaplains to students or young-adult groups. We note the Holy Father's tribute to the promising apostolate which brings together married couples who desire to communicate their experiences to other married couples and thus become apostles of fidelity to the divine law and guides to fulfillment in love.

Education of Children in Sexuality

In accordance with the *Decree on Christian Education* of Vatican Council II we affirm the value and necessity of wisely planned education of children in human sexuality, adapted to the maturity and background of our young people. We are under a grave obligation, in part arising from the new circumstances of modern culture and communications, to assist the family in its efforts to provide such training. This obligation can be met either by systematic provision of such education in the diocesan school curriculum or by the inauguration of acceptable educational programs under other diocesan auspices, including the Confraternity of Christian Doctrine. Parents are those primarily responsible for imparting to their children an awareness of the sacredness of sexuality; this will ordinarily be best accomplished when both parents discharge this duty in mutual consultation and shared responsibility. The necessity for greater communication and cooperation between parents and teachers is highlighted in this problem; the consequent role of Parent-Teacher Guilds and similar home-school associations is apparent.

Parents are sometimes fearful that their right to teach the norms of sexual morality to their children may be usurped or that programs such as we envision may lead to the sexual misdirection of their children if the teachers involved are inadequately prepared or emotionally immature. In the light of such legitimate concerns, the careful selection of instructors for these discussions is a serious responsibility to be shared by priests, school authorities and parents, perhaps best under the auspices of parent-teacher associations.

The content of these instructions should provide an appreciation of "the true values of life and of the family" (*Humanae Vitae*, 21), in addition to a healthy inculcation, from the earliest years of moral and intellectual formation, of how conjugal love involves a harmonious response from the emotions, the passions, the body and the mind. At the same time, healthy Christian attitudes toward life will be developed in young

people if they are given an understanding, consistent with their years, of why the Council insists that those "actions within marriage by which the couple are united intimately and chastely are noble and worthy ones" (*Gaudium et Spes*, 49).

During these early years of physical growth and spiritual formation, especially throughout adolescence, our young people and their neighbors should be taught to appreciate the heroic witness to divine life and the unique service to human life given by those who, with love undivided, dedicate to God and their fellow-men the consecration of their celibacy and virginity for the sake of the Kingdom of God. Our priests, religious brothers and sisters have bound themselves to live in persevering single-hearted commitment as intimate collaborators with God Himself, from Whom every family, whether spiritual or natural, takes its name both in heaven and on earth (Eph. 3,15). Every family is therefore in their debt: the families from which they come, the families to which they bear their special witness of life and love, the national family they strengthen, the family of the Church. No one knows this more than their bishops; no one is more grateful.

The New Family

In facing current problems of the American family, we welcome the open approach of the *Pastoral Constitution on the Church in the Modern World* toward marriage and the family. It provides a timely and optimistic overview of the community aspect of marriage, a community that functions best when all its members understand that freedom is their birthright and a developing sense of responsibity their challenge: It sets up balances which provide for the more perfect personal development of each family member and, at the same time, assures the optimum effect of the family unit in the larger family of man. It recognizes the continual and rapid changes which characterize our times.

The style of family living is undoubtedly affected by changing social conditions, yet the family retains a resilience and strength that help it adapt to change. In fact, the family has always been the witness to change as it passes on the wisdom, successes and accomplishments of one generation to the next as a patrimony for the pursuance of its dreams.

Commenting on this adaptability to change that is almost inherent in the family, Pope Paul VI notes that "in a world in the midst of change, it would be useless to want to close one's eyes to the adaptations which even the most stable, most traditional institutions must accept. No matter how great the merits of the family of yesterday may have been, it is the one of today and of tomorrow which must attract the attention of men who are really preoccupied with the welfare of humanity. These 'new families' possess many new characteristics, some of which may certainly give rise to legitimate disquietude. But—we say without fear—the Church looks with pleasure upon many of these innovations: the cessation, for example, of certain social or family restrictions, the freer and more conscious choice of a spouse, the greater stress placed upon the development of husband and wife, the more lively interest in the education of children, and still many other traits which it is not possible to enumerate in detail" (Paul VI to IUFO).

One of the best examples of this new type of family structure is the present-day American family. It is a community of individual persons joined by human love, and living a community life that provides for the greatest expression of individualism. At the same time, equalitarian marriage patterns have so developed among Americans as to avoid rigid role assignments within the family and thus make possible a deeper family unit.

The family unit develops apart from the parent-families, yet not totally isolated. In our technological culture, transportation facilities and communications media provide new systems of mobility and yet fortunately allow for a strengthening of human bonds among families, despite the distances in geographical location.

The educational attainment of women and a new emphasis on legal and social equality between men and women create further tensions but also opportunities for more effective partnership in marriage. This adds a further reason why a Catholic theology of family life must be spelled out to match the changing patterns of the American family. A relevant theology will reinforce the efforts of spouses to achieve conjugal maturity; it will enable them to realize the more profoundly the difference between romance and love and to understand that only gradually will they achieve the harmony between healthy individualism and mutual self-giving in which Christian personalism consists.

New Tensions, New Needs

Technological and cultural changes bring with them complexities not easily resolved. Some of these set up pressures on the family from outside, some from within. For example, even the family today finds itself under the necessity to develop new channels of "communication"; this seems a formidable word to describe relations within the intimate community that a human family should be. However, the problem is made real by the profoundly changed circumstances under which each family member now seeks to establish an identity while preserving a warm sense of family unity and pride. Family harmony in our day will depend on just such "communication" as parents attempt to solve the authority-obedience dilemma with their growing children. Moreover, reformed "communication" within the family is needed if the manifold educational resources of family life itself are to complement the formal schooling of children.

The individual family is now challenged to new responsibilities toward the plurality of families which comprises the nation, the human community and the Church. And so Christian families, conscious of their part in the progress of the wider human family, will wish to share not only their spiritual heritage with families less privileged but also their material resources. They will seek by their own initiatives to supplement government action, being painfully aware that in our own country many families are victims of poverty, disease and inadequate living standards.

Informed social critics are asserting that family instability in the urban areas of America is the result, in part at least, of our national failure to adopt comprehensive and realistic family-centered policies during the course of this century. The break-down of the family has intrinsic causes, some of them moral, but these have been aggravated by the indifference or neglect of society and by the consequences of poverty and racist attitudes. The object of wise social policy is not only the physical well-being of persons but their emotional stability and moral growth, not as individuals but, whenever possible, within family units.

In principle, American social theory has always recognized that the normal family enjoys a real autonomy; only the abnormal inadequacy of a particular family places its members within the competency of our courts. Even then, whenever possible, it is the disposition of our public agencies to supply the defects of nature by providing the neglected, delinquent or homeless child with the nearest possible approach to life and training in a family setting. Americans have tended to prefer, particularly recently, the plan of foster homes where the role of natural parents can be somehow supplied in the development of the person within a human family. Our theory in all these respects has been admirable; its implementation in legislation and in practice has not always kept pace with the problems testing the theory. The present urban crisis is but one evidence of this.

Though families, like man himself, do not live on bread alone, without bread they suffer and die. Food programs still need a family orientation. Poor housing, for further example, has an adverse effect on family stability. We urge an expansion of home ownership programs for low- and moderate-income families, especially the larger families frequently neglected in these plans, as well as programs for low-rent housing and housing rehabilitation.

Programs devised to assist less advantaged familes should at all costs avoid disruption of the family unit. A major disruption occurs when mothers are required to separate themselves from their young children for the sake of added income. Disruption has too often been the result of certain welfare policies which, whether consciously intended or not, have destroyed rather than supported family stability; one such policy we pinpointed in our reference to the "man in the house" rule when we spoke in a recent statement on the national social problem, bot others could be documented. Every member of each family has a right to be cared for, not as an isolated person but as a person who belongs with and depends upon a family. We therefore favor the trend to consider social service programs, domestic relations courts and child welfare casework as involving family rather than merely individual dimensions and solutions.

Whenever a family is undermined, society suffers the loss. There are no insignificant families, as there is no insignificant person. If families are to function as the good of society requires, each must have income proportionate to its needs.

Wages in our country are usually based upon the work done, plus productivity. Little or no consideration is given to the family situation of the individual, his marital status, or the number of children in his home. It should not normally be necessary for the father of a family to "moonlight," seeking employment from more than one source to support his wife and children. Single men and the married men with families receive the same rates of pay for the same work. As a result, one sector of the population bears a disproportionately large share of the financial budren of maintaining the child population, which means the future nation, except for income tax benefits, which may unfortunately be cancelled out by consumer taxes. The effective solution we are urging may well require a family allowance system in the United States similar to those adopted by Canada, many European nations, Australia, New Zealand and some governments of South America. We stand ready to support enlightened legislation in this sense.

The challenges and threats to contemporary family life may often seem insuperable. However, the resources of this nation are more than sufficient to enhance the security and prosperity of our families at home while leaving us free to fulfill our duties in charity and justice abroad. The scientific, educational and financial resources of our nation cannot be better utilized than in defense and development of the family. The future of civilization itself depends upon such creative use of our resources.

Our concern with improved social conditions and public policies protective of the family includes recognition of the special merits of some families. We second the tribute of the Council's *Pastoral Constitution* to parents of large families; we add a further tribute to those parents who, in a tradition that has been the strength of American Catholicism, have provided their children, very often at great sacrifice, with educational opportunities under religious auspices from pre-school years to higher education.

We are mindful of those families which include disadvantaged children and of families which by adoption assume full responsibility for children not born to them. Adoption corresponds with a deeply human instinct it gives a home to the homeless and parents to the orphaned while at the same time rewarding the love with which a family welcomes life not originally committed to its keeping.

Likewise praiseworthy is the unselfishness which prompts qualified people to become foster parents to children who need material, emotional or spiritual assistance at some point in their lives. Finally, we offer a word of encouragement to our brothers or sisters in Christ who care for children in one-parent families. The sacrifices required to provide for the physical welfare and psychological development of children under these circumstances are sometimes extraordinary. Those who thus spend themselves on behalf of life and love witness to the world and the Church a generosity which cannot fail to inspire others and to sanctify themselves.

Further Threats to Life

At this tense moment in our history when external wars and internal violence make us so conscious of death, an affirmation of the sanctity of human life by renewed attention to the family is imperative. Let society always be on the side of life. Let it never dictate, directly or indirectly, recourse to the prevention of life or to its destruction in any of its phases; neither let it require as a condition of economic assistance that any family yield conscientious determination of the number of its children to the decision of persons or agencies outside the family.

Stepped-up pressures for moral and legal acceptance of directly procured abortion make necessary pointed reference to this threat to the right of life. Reverence for life demands freedom from direct interruption of life once it is conceived. Conception initiates a process whose purpose is the realization of human personality. A human person, nothing more and nothing less, is always at issue once conception has taken place. We expressly repudiate any contradictory suggestion as contrary to Judaeo-Christian traditions inspired by love for life, and Anglo-Saxon legal traditions protective of life and the person.

Abortion brings to an end with irreversible finality both the existence and the destiny of the developing human person. Conscious of the inviolability of life, the Second Vatican Council teaches:

"God, the Lord of life, has conferred on man the surpassing ministry of safeguarding life, a ministry which must be ful-filled in a manner that is worthy of man. Therefore, from the moment of its conception life must be guarded with the greatest care while abortion and infanticide are unspeakable crimes" (*Gaudium et Spes,* 51).

The judgment of the Church on the evil of terminating life derives from the Christian awareness that men are not the masters but the ministers of life. Hence, the Council declares: ". . . whatever is opposed to life itself, such as any type of murder, genocide, abortion, euthanasia, or willful self-destruction, whatever violates the integrity of the human person . . . all these things and others of their like are infamies indeed. They poison human society but they do more harm to those who practice them than those who suffer from the injury. Moreover, they are a supereme dishonor to the Creator" (*Gaudium et Spes,* 27).

A Note of Christian Optimism

Pressing concerns of the hour have led us to consider with you many of the problems of family life, together with a Christian appraisal of them. The family is, however, much more than the sum of its problems. It is, as we said earlier, the place where the person occurs, where life begins, where fidelity and hope are nourished, where human love reaches its most intense expression. The family is, indeed, that "school of deeper humanity" of which the Vatican Council speaks (*Gaudium et Spes,* 52).

The Christian family is an image of God and a sign of the Church. It is the community wherein Christ is most powerfully preached, where Christians first hear the name of God, first learn to pray, and first express their faith. In the words and example of their believing parents, children come to know what faith is and how it must be lived, what life is and how it must be honored. For this reason, a spirituality which is suitable to the contemporary family and which brings all members of the family together in faith and hope is, we repeat, the most urgent need of modern culture.

Since the family is the basic unit of human society, it should be the object of civilization's most enlightened concern. Since it is the basic unit of their life, parishes should make the needs of the family and the benefits which the family brings to the parish controlling norms in the planning of parish organizations and activities, liturgical, educational, charitable and social.

As bishops of the Catholic Church in the United States, concerned for her present well-being and prospects, our first prayer is for the families who comprise her parishes and dioceses. Our optimisim for the future of the Church, the family of God, springs largely from optimism for the future of the family. In turn, our basis for optimism for the future of family life, despite occasional negative signs, rests upon the persevering hope of married couples whose responsibility to life and vocation to love have been the opening theme of this pastoral letter.

As last year we saluted priests, for their special part in the work of God, so this year we salute Christian spouses who, "made to the image of the living God and enjoying the authentic dignity of persons, are joined to one another in equal affection, harmony of mind and the work of mutual sanctification. Thus, following Christ Who is the principle of life, by the sacrifices and joys of their vocation and through their faithful love, [they have] become witnesses of the mystery of love which the Lord revealed to the world by His dying and His rising up to live again" (*Gaudium et Spes,* 52).

The Family of Nations

We share the deep concern of thoughtful people in our times, a concern voiced by the Vatican Council, that "the whole human family has reached an hour of supreme crisis" (*Gaudium et Spes*, 77). The crisis can ultimately offer great promise for a more abundant human life, but at the moment it portends grave threats to all life. The threats to life depend on urgent and difficult decisions concerning war and peace. In considering these we share the conviction of Vatican Council II that the horror and perversity of technological warfare "compel us to undertake an evaluation of war with an entirely new attitude."

This compelling obligation is the greater in our case since we are citizens of a nation in many ways the most powerful in the world. The responsibility of moral leadership is the greater in the local Church of a nation whose arsenals contain the greatest nuclear potential for both the harm that we would wish to impede or the help it is our obligation to encourage. We are acutely aware that our moral posture and comportment in this hour of supreme crisis will be assessed by the judgment of history and of God.

We renew the affirmation by the Council that "the loftier strivings and aspirations of the human race are in harmony with the message of the Gospel" (n. 77). We speak as witnesses to that Gospel, aware that the issues of war and peace test the relevancy of its message for our generation, particularly in terms of the service of life and its dignity. We seek to speak in the spirit of that Gospel message, which is at heart a doctrine of non-violence rather than violence, of peace understood as Jesus proclaimed it (cf. Jn. 14,27).

We call upon American Catholics to evaluate war with that "entirely new attitude" for which the Council appealed and which may rightly be expected of all who, calling themselves Christians, proclaim their identity with the Prince of Peace. We share with all men of good will the conviction that a more humane society will not come "unless each person devotes himself with renewed determination to the cause of peace" (n. 77). We appeal to policy makers and statesmen to reflect soberly on the Council teaching concerning peace and war, and vigorously to pursue the search for means by which at all times to limit and eventually to outlaw the destructiveness of war.

The Vatican Council noted that "war continues to produce daily devastation in one or another part of the world" (n. 79). The observation has lost none of its truth in the period since the Council ended; indeed, there have been further grievous outbreaks of war and aggression.

Of one mind with the Council, we condemn without qualification wars of aggression however their true character may sometimes be veiled. Whatever case there may have seemed to exist in other times for wars fought for the domination of another nation, such a case can no longer be imagined given the circumstances of modern warfare, the heightened sense of international mutuality and the increasingly available humane means to the realization of that mutuality.

We join wholeheartedly in the Council's condemnation of wars fought without limitation. We recognize the right of legitimate self-defense and, in a world society still unorganized, the necessity for recourse to armed defense and to collective security action in the absence of a competent authority on the international level and once peaceful means

have been exhausted. But we seek to limit warfare and to humanize it, where it remains a last resort, in the maximum degree possible. Most of all, we urge the enlisting of the energies of all men of good will in forging the instruments of peace, to the end that war may at long last be outlawed.

Meanwhile, we are gratefully conscious that "those who are pledged to the service of their country as members of its armed forces should regard themselves as agents of security and freedom on behalf of their people. As long as they fulfill this role properly, they are making a genuine contribution to the establishment of peace" (*Gaudium et Spes*, 79).

In the Christian message peace is not merely the absence of war. Ultimately, of course, it presupposes that presence within and among men of a positive principle of life and unity which is none other than the divine life to which the Church bears witness, of which Christ in His Church is the source. The soul, then, of a peaceful society is divine charity. But justice, the great concern of the well-ordered State and the justification for its existence, is the foundation of the organized society.

Therefore, peace cannot be reduced solely to the maintenance of a balance of power between enemies; nor is it to be brought about by dictatorship, whether this be the imposition of the sheer will of a ruler, a party or even a majority. It is an enterprise of justice and must be built up ceaselessly in seeking to satisfy the all-embracing demands of the common good. This is the point of Pope Paul's positive, dynamic concept of peace: the modern word for peace is development. Peace therefore presupposes the fraternal confidence which manifests itself in a firm determination to respect other persons and peoples, above all their human dignity, and to collaborate with them in the pursuit of the shared hopes of mankind.

Arms Control

It is in nuclear warfare, even in its "cold" phase or form, that mankind confronts the moral issue of modern war in its extreme case. This has become a situation in which two adversaries possess and deploy weapons which, if used against each other, could annihilate their respective civilizations and even threaten the survival of the human race. Nothing more dramatically suggests the anti-life direction of technological warfare than the neutron bomb; one philosopher declares that the manner in which it would leave entire cities intact, but totally without life, makes it, perhaps, the symbol of our civilization. It would be perverse indeed if the Christian conscience were to be unconcerned or mute in the face of the multiple moral aspects of these awesome prospects.

It is now a quarter century since Pope Pius XII summoned that conscience to a "War on War." He pointed out World War II's "unspeakable atrocities," the "image of a hell upon which anyone who nourishes humane sentiments in his heart can have no more ardent wish than to close the door forever." He warned against the further progress of "human inventions . . . directed to destruction," and pleaded that to the recognition of the immorality of wars of aggression there be added "the threat of a judicial intervention of the nations and of a punishment inflicted on the aggressor by the United Nations, so that war may always feel itself proscribed, always under the watchful guard of preventive action." He argued that then "humanity, issuing from the dark night in which it has been submerged for so great a length of time, will be able to greet the dawn of a new and better era in its history" (Christmas broadcast, 1944).

The Second Vatican Council, in a solemn declaration, endorsed "the condemnation of total warfare issued by recent popes" and stated:

"Every act of war directed to the indiscriminate destruction of whole cities or vast areas with their inhabitants is a crime against God and man which merits firm and unequivocal condemnation" (*Gaudium et Spes, 80*).

The Council explicitly condemned the use of weapons of mass destruction, but abstained from condemning the *possession* of such weapons to deter "possible enemy attack (n. 81). Though not passing direct judgment on this strategy of deterrence, the Council did declare that "men should be convinced that the arms race in which so many countries are engaged is not a safe way to preserve a steady peace. Nor is the so-called 'balance' resulting from this race a pure and authentic peace. Rather than being eliminated thereby, the causes of war threaten to grow gradually stronger . . . Therefore it must be said again: the arms race is an utterly treacherous trap for humanity, and one which ensnares the poor to an intolerable degree" (n. 81).

The Council did not call for unilateral disarmament; Christian morality is not lacking in realism. But it did call for reciprocal or collective disarmament "proceeding at an equal pace according to agreement and backed up by authentic and workable safeguards" (n. 82). There are hopeful signs that such a formula may be strengthened by the Partial Test Ban Treaty and that the commitment under the Non-Proliferation Treaty to proceed to a negotiation of balanced reductions of nuclear weapons—at the same time extending the use of nuclear power for peaceful development of the needy nations under adequate inspection safeguards—may provide a positive, sane pattern for the future. We earnestly pray so, commending the furtherance of these hopes to responsible political leaders and to the support of all citizens.

Meanwhile, it is greatly to be desired that such prospects not be dashed by irrational resolves to keep ahead in "assured destruction" capability. Rather it is to be hoped that the early ratification by the Senate of the Non-Proliferation Treaty—which in essence is a Treaty between the USSR and the US and other nations—will hasten discussion of across-the-board reductions by the big powers. Despite, and even because of, the provocations in Eastern Europe and elsewhere, the United States should continue steps to create a better climate for these discussions, such as taking the lead in inviting the UN Atomic Energy Commission and other organizations and foreign States to visit its nuclear facilities, and scrupulously reviewing all commitments for the sale, loan or lease of armaments.

The Council's position on the arms race was clear. To recall it: "Therefore, we declare once again: the arms race is an utterly treacherous trap for humanity . . . It is much to be feared that if this race persists, it will eventually spawn all the lethal ruin whose path it is now making ready" (n. 81).

Nonetheless, the nuclear race goes on. The latest act in the continuing nuclear arms race is no doubt the US decision to build a "thin" anti-ballistic missile system to defend against possible nuclear attack by another world power. This decision has been widely interpreted as the prelude to a "thick" ABM system to defend against possible nuclear attack.

In themselves, such anti-ballistic missiles are purely defensive, designed to limit the damage to the United States from nuclear attack. Nevertheless, by upsetting the present strategic balance, the so-called balance of terror, there is grave danger that a United States ABM system will incite other nations to increase their offensive nuclear forces with the seeming excuse of a need to restore the balance.

Despite the danger of triggering an expanded escalation of the arms race the pressures for a "thick" ABM deployment persist.

We seriously question whether the present policy of maintaining nuclear superiority is meaningful for security. There is no advantage to be gained by nuclear superiority, however it is computed, when each side is admittedly capable of inflicting overwhelming damage on the other, even after being attacked first. Such effective parity has been operative for some years. Any effort to achieve superiority only leads to ever-higher levels of armaments as it forces the side with the lesser capability to seek to maintain its superiority. In the wake of this action-reaction phenomenon comes a decrease in both stability and security.

The National Conference of Catholic Bishops pledges its united effort toward forming a climate of public opinion for peace, mindful of the Council's advice that "government officials . . . depend on public opinion and feeling to the greatest possible extent" (n. 82). We will therefore, through existing and improved agencies, support national programs of education for Catholic Americans and for all Americans in collaboration with all religious groups and other organizations.

With *Gaudium et Spes*, we commend the arduous and unceasing efforts of statesmen and specialists in the field of arms control and disarmament, and add our own encouragement of systematic studies in this field. As the Council appealed to Catholic scholars throughout the world to participate more fully in such studies, so we call upon intellectuals in the Church in our land to bring scholarly competence and their powers of persuasion to that "war on war" which the modern Popes have without exception pleaded that we wage.

We urge Catholics, and indeed all our countrymen, to make a ceaseless vigil of prayers for peace and for all those who are charged with the delicate and difficult negotiations of disarmament. Such prayers provide the most obvious and appropriate occasion for ecumenical services bringing together all in our communities who cherish the blessed vision of peace heralded by the Hebrew prophets and preached by Christ and His Apostles. We cannot but question the depth of the commitment to peace of people of religious background who no longer pray for peace. But those who only pray for peace, leaving to others the arduous work for peace, the dialogue for peace, have a defective theology concerning the relation between human action and the accomplishment of that will of God in which is our peace. So, too, those who, neglectful of the part of prayer, rely only on their own power, or on the pooling of merely human resources on intelligence, energy and even good will, forget the wisdom of Scripture: "If the Lord does not build the house, in vain the masons toil; if the Lord does not guard the city, in vain the sentries watch" (Ps. 127, 1-2).

The International Community

The Council Fathers recognized that not even ending the nuclear arms race, which itself cannot be accomplished without the full cooperation of the international community, would ensure the permanent removal of the awesome threat of modern war. Nor would disarmament alone, even assuming it to be complete and across the board, remove the causes of war. "This goal undoubtedly requires the establishment of some universal public authority acknowledged as such by all, and endowed with effective power to safeguard, on the behalf of all, security, regard for justice and respect for rights" (n. 82).

Such an authority, furthermore, is required by the growing, ever more explicit interdependence of all men and nations as a result of which the common good "today takes on an increasingly universal complexion and consequently involves rights and duties with respect to the whole human race" (n. 82).

Therefore political leaders should ". . . extend their thoughts and their spirit beyond the confines of their own nation, put aside national selfishness and ambition to dominate other nations, and nourish a profound reverence for the whole of humanity, which is already making its way so laboriously toward greater unity" (n. 82).

We commend the efforts of world statesmen, particularly those of our own nation, who seek to extend the spirit and practice of cooperation in international agencies and regional associations of nations, with the object not only of terminating or preventing war, and of building up a body of international law, but also of removing the causes of war through positive programs.

Since war remains a melancholy fact of life today, we believe the United States not only should insist on adherence to and the application by all nations of existing international conventions or treaties on the laws of war, such as the revised Geneva Convention relative to the treatment of prisoners of war, but should take the lead in seeking to update them. Certain forms of warfare, new and old, should be outlawed, and practices in dealing with civilian populations, prisoners of war and refugees are always in need of review and reform.

Here, too, our dependence on responsible writers, informed speakers and competent critics is crucial to the cause of peace. Hence we encourage Catholic scholars to undertake systematic studies of new developments, theories and practices in warfare, including guerilla warfare, revolution and "wars of liberation." Changing political patterns, improved techniques of communication, new methods of remote controls and of surveillance of individuals and communities alike made possible by science, as well as shifting ethical standards, make it the vocation of devout intellectuals, both as citizens of their own nations and servants of the common good of mankind, to bring informed competence to the illumination, discussion and resolution of the complex issues, many of them moral, arising from all these.

A Catholic position of opposition to compulsory peacetime military service, first formulated on the level of the Holy See by Pope Benedict XV, has had for its premise the fact that such service has been a contributing cause of the breeding of actual wars, a part of the "great armaments" and "armed peace" security concept, and, in the words of Cardinal Gasparri in a letter to Lloyd George, the cause of such great evils for more than a century that the cure of these evils can only be found in the suppression of this system. In the spirit of this position, we welcome the voices lifted up among our political leaders which ask for a total review of the draft system and the establishment of voluntary military service in a professional army with democratic safeguards and for clear purposes of adequate defense. Our call for the end of any draft system at home which, in practice, amounts at times to compulsory peacetime military service is in direct line with previous resolutions of the hierarchy of the United States on compulsory military training (c. *Our Bishops Speak,* pp. 234, 237).

Apart from the question of war itself, we deem it opportune here to reiterate the Council's condemnation of genocide, the methodical extermination of an entire people, nation or ethnic minority for reasons connected with race, religion or status such as that undertaken by the Nazis against the Jews among their own citizens and later against all the Jewish people, as well as so-called "gypsies." We would urge United States ratification of the United Nations Convention on this subject and of every other sound implementing instrument by which the United Nations Declaration of Human Rights can be translated from the level of ideals to that of actuality. Furthermore, we urge increased support by our own countrymen and citizens of all nations of all international programs consistent with the protection and promotion of the sanctity of human life and the dignity of the human person in times of war and peace.

We earnestly appeal to our own government and to all governments to give the elimination of the present international "war system" a priority consistent with the damaging effect of massive armament programs on all the objectives of the good society to which enlightened governments give priorities: education, public health, a true sense of security, prosperity, maximum liberty, the flourishing of the humane arts and sciences, in a word the service of life itself. Thus can we strive to move away, as reason and religion demand, from the "war system" to an international system in which unilateral recourse to force is increasingly restricted.

This will require international peace-making and peace-keeping machinery. To this end we urge all to support efforts for a stronger and more effective United Nations that it may become a true instrument of peace and justice among nations. In this respect the peace motivation of Pope Paul's public support of the United Nations by his moral authority and teaching office at the time of his visit to that body on its anniversary should be normative for Catholics.

We would welcome in official pronouncements of our own and other governments, as well as in the increased support given to the United Nations and associated agencies by the citizens of all nations, a greater interest in and direction toward the establishment of that universal public authority which the Council Fathers urged.

We recognize that any use of police action by such an international authority, or, in the meantime, by the UN as presently constituted, or by duly constituted regional agencies, must be carefully subject to covenants openly arrived at and freely accepted, covenants spelling out clear norms such as that of proportionate force; here, again, the work of qualified and conscientious specialists is indispensable.

Turning to the more positive aspects of the building of an international community and the duties of us as Americans in this matter, we deplore the lack of a stable, persevering national concern for the promotion of the international common good. This is reflected in the fickleness of public interest in and Congressional support of foreign aid. It is reflected also in a seeming insensitivity to the importance of trade agreements beneficial to developing nations. A like lack of generosity, dangerous to the fully human common good, is present in the increasingly bold linking of contraceptive programs, even when superficially voluntary, to needed aid programs. Future aid and trade assistance programs should become increasingly multilateral; they should never merely serve national self-interest except to the extent that national interest is genuinely part and parcel of the general good of the human community.

Because of the war in Vietnam, and the growing preoccupation with the social problems of our cities, there is the peril of an upsurge of exaggerated forms of nationalism and isolationism which the teachings of all Churches reprove and the experiences of World War II had, we hoped, forever discredited.

It is the duty of our political leadership, of citizens and especially of believers who acknowledge the brotherhood of man, to promote and develop the spirit of international concern, cooperation and understanding.

As the Council noted, ". . . there arises a surpassing need for renewed education of attitudes and for new inspiration in the area of public opinion. Those who are dedicated to the work of education, particularly of the young, or who mold public opinion should regard as their most weighty task the effort to instruct all in fresh sentiments of peace" (n. 82).

To assist the agencies and institutions of the Catholic Church in the United States in their response to this "most weighty task," the Catholic Bishops have recently established a Division of World Justice and Peace, corresponding to the newly established Vatican Commission. It is our desire that the Division will stimulate renewed efforts in this field, and coordinate whenever possible such efforts with those of other Christian bodies in an ecumenical framework. We call upon all men of conscience, all public spirited citizens, to dedicate themselves with fresh energy to this work.

We believe that the talents and resources of our land are so abundant that we may promote the common good of nations at no expense to the vitally necessary works of urban and rural reconstruction in our own country. The latter are the first order of domestic policy, just as the former should be the first order of foreign policy. Neither should be neglected, both being equally urgent; in the contemporary and developing world order their fortunes are intertwined.

Vietnam

In a previous statement we ventured a tentative judgment that, on balance, the U.S. presence in Vietnam was useful and justified.

Since then American Catholics have entered vigorously into the national debate on this question, which, explicitly or implicitly, is going deeply into the moral aspects of our involvement in Vietnam. In this debate, opinions among Catholics appear as varied as in our society as a whole; one cannot accuse Catholics of either being partisans of any one point of view or of being unconcerned. In our democratic system the fundamental right of political dissent cannot be denied, nor is rational debate on public policy decisions of government in the light of moral and political principles to be discouraged. It is the duty of the governed to analyze responsibly the concrete issues of public policy.

In assessing our country's involvement in Vietnam we must ask: Have we already reached, or passed, the point where the principle of proportionality becomes decisive? How much more of our resources in men and money should we commit to this struggle, assuming an acceptable cause or intention? Has the conflict in Vietnam provoked inhuman dimensions of suffering? Would not an untimely withdrawal be equally disastrous?

Granted that financial considerations are necessarily subordinate to ethical values in any moral question, nonetheless many wonder if perhaps a measure of the proportions in this, as in any modern war, may be reflected in the amounts inevitably lost to education, poverty-relief and positive works of social justice at home and abroad (including Southeast Asia) as a result of the mounting budgets for this and like military operations. This point has frequently been raised by the Popes, notably by Pope Pius XII who invoked the principle of proportionality in his analysis of the morality even of defensive wars, particularly when these involve A.B.C. elements (atomic, biological, chemical) and losses disproportionate to the "injustice tolerated" (Address to Military Doctors, Oct. 19, 1953).

While it would be beyond our competence to propose any technical formulas for bringing the Vietnam War to an end, we welcome the bombing halt and pray for the success of the negotiations now underway.

Meanwhile there are moral lessons to be learned from our involvement in Vietnam that will apply to future cases. One might be that military power and technology do not suffice, even with the strongest resolve, to restore order or accomplish peace. As a rule internal political conflicts are too complicated to be solved by the external application of force and technology.

Another might be the realization that some evils existing in the world, evils such as undernutrition, economic frustration, social stagnation and political injustices, may be more readily attacked and corrected through non-military means, than by military efforts to counteract the subversive forces bent on their exploitation.

In addition, may we not hope that violence will be universally discredited as a means of remedying human ills, and that the spirit of love "may overcome the barriers that divide, cherish the bonds of mutual charity, understand others and pardon those who have done them wrong"? (*Pacem in Terris*, Article 171).

The Role of Conscience

The war in Vietnam typifies the issues which present and future generations will be less willing to leave entirely to the normal political and bureaucratic processes of national decision-making. It is not surprising that those who are most critical, even intemperate in their discussion of war as an instrument of national policy or as a ready means to the settling even of wrongs, are among the young; the burden of killing and dying falls principally on them.

There is sometimes ground for questions as to whether the attitudes of some toward military duty do not spring from cowardice. In this problem, as in all crises which test generosity and heroism, cases of moral as well as physical cowardice doubtless occur. But a blanket charge of this kind would be unfair to those young people who are clearly willing to suffer social ostracism and even prison terms because of their opposition to a particular war. One must conclude that for many of our youthful protesters, the motives spring honestly from a principled opposition to a given war as pointless or immoral.

Nor can it be said that such conscientious objection to war, as war is waged in our times, is entirely the result of subjective considerations and without reference to the message of the Gospel and the teaching of the Church; quite the contrary, frequently conscientious dissent reflects the influence of the principles which inform modern papal teaching, the Pastoral Constitution and a classical tradition of moral doctrine in the Church, including, in fact, the norms for the moral evaluation of a theoretically just war.

The enthusiasm of many young people for new programs of service to fellow humans in need may be proof that some traditional forms of patriotism are in process of being supplemented by a new spirit of dedication to humanity and to the moral prestige of one's own nation. This new spirit must be taken seriously; it may not always match the heroism of the missionaries and the full measure of the life of faith, but it is not contradictory to these and may open up new forms of Christian apostolate.

As witnesses to a spiritual tradition which accepts enlightened conscience, even when honestly mistaken, as the immediate arbiter of moral decisions, we can only feel reassured by this evidence of individual responsibility and the decline of uncritical conformism to patterns some of which included strong moral elements, to be sure, but also included political, social, cultural and like controls not necessarily in conformity with the mind and heart of the Church.

If war is ever to be outlawed, and replaced by more humane and enlightened institutions to regulate conflicts among nations, institutions rooted in the notion of universal common good, it will be because the citizens of this and other nations have rejected the tenets of exaggerated nationalism and insisted on principles of non-violent political and civic action in both the domestic and international spheres.

We therefore join with the Council Fathers in praising "those who renounce the use of violence in the vindication of their rights and who resort to methods of defense which are otherwise available to weaker parties, provided that this can be done without injury to the rights and duties of others or of the community itself" (n. 78).

It is in this light that we seek to interpret and apply to our own situation the advice of the Vatican Council on the treatment of conscientious objectors. The Council endorsed laws that

"make humane provision for the care of those who for reasons of conscience refuse to bear arms, provided, however, that they accept some other form of service to the human community" (n. 79).

The present laws of this country, however, provide only for those whose reasons of conscience are grounded in a total rejection of the use of military force. This form of conscientious objection deserves the legal provision made for it, but we consider that the time has come to urge that similar consideration be given those whose reasons of conscience are more personal and specific.

We therefore recommend a modification of the Selective Service Act making it possible, although not easy, for so-called selective conscientious objectors to refuse—without fear of imprisonment or loss of citizenship—to serve in wars which they consider unjust or in branches of service (e.g., the strategic nuclear forces) which would subject them to the performance of actions contrary to deeply held moral convictions about indiscriminate killing. Some other form of service to the human community should be required of those so exempted.

Whether or not such modifications in our laws are in fact made, we continue to hope that, in the all-important issue of war and peace, all men will follow their consciences. We can do no better than to recall, as did the Vatican Council, "the permanent binding force of universal natural law and its all embracing principles," to which "man's conscience itself gives ever more emphatic voice."

In calling so persistently in this Pastoral for studies on the application of sound moral principles to new dimensions of changes in the problems of war and peace, we are mindful of our own responsibility to proclaim the Gospel of peace and to teach the precepts of both natural and revealed divine law concerning the establishing of peace everywhere on earth (n. 79). We therefore make our own the Council's judgment on "the deeper causes of war," sins like envy, mistrust and egoism. We echo the warning given by Pope Paul at the United Nations:

"Today as never before, in an era marked by such human progress, there is need for an appeal to the moral conscience of man. For the danger comes not from progress, nor from science—on the contrary, if properly utilized these could resolve many of the grave problems which beset mankind. The real danger comes from man himself, who has at his disposal ever more powerful instruments, which can be used as well for destruction as for the loftiest conquests."

The hour has indeed struck for "conversion" for personal transformation, for interior renewal. We must once again begin to think of man in a new way, and of human life with a new appreciation of its worth, its dignity and its call to elevation to the level of the life of God Himself. All this requires that, with refreshed purpose and deepened faith, we follow the urging of St. Paul that we "put on the new man, which has been created according to God in justice and holiness of truth" (Eph. 4, 23).

Conclusion

Christians believe God to be the "source of life" (cf. Jn. 5,26) and of love since "love comes from God" (cf. 1 Jn. 4,7). "God is love" (1 Jn. 4,8) and man has been made in His image and likeness (Gen. 1,26). Thus, man is most himself when he honors life and lives by love. Then he is most like to God.

The doctrine and defense of life require a renewed spirituality in the Church. Such a spirituality will reaffirm the sacred character of married love through which life is begun, the dignity of the family within which love brings life to maturity, and the blessed vision of peace in which life is shared by men and nations in a world community of love.

These themes, all of which touch on life, we have explored in terms of the family, the commonwealth of nations and some of the anti-life forces which threaten these.

In her defense of human life the Church in our day makes her own, as did Moses, the words by which God Himself reduces our perplexities to a clear, inescapable choice:

"I call heaven and earth to witness against you this day, that I have set before you life and death . . . therefore, choose life that you and your descendants may live . . ." (Deut. 30,19).

The author

Father Padovano was born on September 18, 1934 in Harrison, New Jersey, attended Seton Hall University and the North American College in Rome. He was ordained, with the Class of 1960 at the North American College and received two graduate degrees in the same year from Roman Universities (S.T.D. and Ph.L.).

Presently, Father Padovano is Professor of Dogmatic Theology at Immaculate Conception Seminary at Darlington, New Jersey, and has taught courses at Villanova, St. Mary's College at Notre Dame and the University of St. Thomas in Houston, Texas. In addition to his teaching, he is a weekend Assistant at a Church in the Archdiocese of Newark and has traveled throughout the country during the past three years giving talks and lectures in almost every State and at almost every major theological and philosophical meeting. Thus during his 9 years in the priesthood he has been active at both the theological and pastoral levels.

Father Padovano has been appointed to: the Archdiocesan Commission for Ecumenical and Inter-religious Affairs; the Commission for Instruction of Clergy in Documents of Vatican II; an elected Delegate-at-Large—Senate of Priests, Archdiocese of Newark; the Editorial Board of The Advocate and Consultor for the National Catholic Office for Radio and Television.

Previously published books: The Estranged God (Sheed and Ward, 1966); Who is Christ? (Ave Maria Press, 1967). Articles published in Magazines: Guide, Catholic World, Ave Maria, Christian Century, National Catholic Reporter, Sign and Preaching. Theological Papers published: Anglican Concept of Episcopacy (1964); Mary, Mother of the Church (1966); American Unbelief and the Death of God (1966, v.21 Proceedings of Catholic Theological Society of America); Original Sin and Christian Anthropology (1967 v.22 Proceedings of Catholic Theological Society of America).